the Idler

ISSUE 38 | WINTER 2006

First published in Great Britain in 2006

10 9 8 7 6 5 4 3 2 1

The Idler, Issue 38
© copyright Idle Limited, 2006

First published by Ebury Press, Random House, 20 Vauxhall Bridge Road,
London SW1V 2SA

Random House Australia (Pty) Limited
20 Alfred Street, Milsons Point, Sydney, New South Wales 2061, Australia
Random House Publishers India Private Limited
301 World Trade Tower, Hotel Intercontinental Grand Complex, Barakhamba
Lane, New Delhi, 110 001 India
Random House New Zealand Limited
18 Poland Road, Glenfield, Auckland 10, New Zealand
Random House South Africa (Pty) Limited
Endulini, 5A Jubilee Road, Parktown 2193, South Africa
The Random House Group Limited Reg. No. 954009
www.randomhouse.co.uk
A CIP catalogue record for this book is available from the British Library.

The views expressed by the contributors do not necessarily reflect
those of the editors.

Cover illustration by Andrew Council
Text design and typesetting by Gavin Pretor-Pinney
Additional layout by Chloe King and Ian Vince

ISBN 0091916496
ISBN 9780091916497
Papers used by Ebury Press are natural, recyclable products made from wood
grown in sustainable forests.

Printed and bound in Germany by Appl, Wemding

Editor: Tom Hodgkinson   Creative Director: Gavin Pretor-Pinney
Deputy Editor: Dan Kieran   Managing Editor: Clare Pollard
Designers: Ian Vince and Chlöe King
Editor at Large: Matthew De Abaitua
Literary Editor: Tony White   Sports Editor: John Moore
Music Editor: Will Hodgkinson   Motoring Editor: Fanny Johnstone
Contributing Editors: Greg Rowland, Ian Vince
For editorial enquiries call 020 7691 0320

WAS JERUSALEM BUILDED HERE?
~ WILLIAM BLAKE

53 Sloane Square, London, SW1X 8AX
Tel: 0207.259.9566.

207 Westbourne Grove, London, W11 2SF
Tel: 0207.731.7490.

33 Amwell Street, London, EC1 1UR
Tel: 0207 833 2367.

www.emmahope.co.uk

CONTENTS THE IDLER *Issue 38, Winter 2006*

THE CLOUDSPOTTER'S GUIDE

GAVIN PRETOR-PINNEY

SCEPTRE

'A lovely book, the sort that everybody should have in the car or
on the kitchen windowsill' *Daily Telegraph*
'Read this eye-opening and amusingly written book' *Daily Mail*

Looking up will never be the same again

WWW.CLOUDAPPRECIATIONSOCIETY.ORG

GIVE UP TV 036

CONTENTS

THE IDLER *Issue 38, Winter 2006*

EDITOR'S LETTER

out there. Just do it. Make a difference. Make your mark on the world.

Well, might it not be that it's all this frantic scurrying around that has caused the problems in the first place? That our urge to meddle, interfere and improve things is precisely what is wrecking the planet? It's our machines and chemicals that are to blame. Could it not be true, then, that the best way of saving the planet might actually be to refrain from action? To withdraw? To let nature get on with it? To do nothing?

This is the idea explored in our Green Man issue, where renowned Gaia

S omething must be done, that is the constant refrain of the reformers. Something must be done to save the planet. Act now. Get

scientist Stephan Harding of Dartington College argues that it is our view of the planet as a resource to be exploited for money that is helping to destroy it. What we need to do, therefore, is a lot more lying around doing nothing. Go and lie on your back on the grass, he says. Stop shopping. Use the car less. Truly, idleness will save the world.

We also meet the shamanistic agitator Jamie Reid, and look back at a career that links punk, druidry, anger and joy. Richard Benson chronicles his attempts to sow a wild flower meadow. John Michellwrites

on good old William Cobbett. Plus we have new cloud pictures from the Cloud Appreciation Society.

And we start the ukulele revolution, with a 16-page special devoted to this most punk of musical instruments. Cheap, easy and very enjoyable to play, it's sure to sweep the nation. I can see it now: large groups of friends lying on their backs in the park, strumming ukuleles together, drinking wine all afternoon.

Forward the revolution!

Tom Hodgkinson
Tom@idler.co.uk

IDLER CONTRIBUTORS

Who are the Idlers?

BADUADE (a person given to idle observation) is otherwise known as Joanna Walsh, and can be found at www.baduade.typepad.com or www.eastwing.co.uk

RICHARD BENSON is the author of *The Farm* (Hamish Hamilton) and is currently working on a new book about Northern working class life in the 1970s.

GRAHAM BURNETT is a permaculture teacher and designer and author of *Permaculture: A Beginner's Guide*, *Earth Writings* and other publications. You can contact him via his website, www.spiralseed.co.uk

MATTHEW DE ABAITUA is always available

MATHEW CLAYTON spends his days working at Ebury Press and his nights playing the baritone ukulele as part of the Dulwich Ukulele Club, www.theduc.org

CLARE DOWDY is writing a book on the best-looking independent shops around the world. This gives her the opportunity to slag off chainstores.

BILL DRUMMOND wants to uke 'em all

HANNAH DYSON draws anthropomorphic creatures and other beings

RACHAEL FIELD produces plays, paints pictures, makes films—and has never done a day's work in her life

GILES GODWIN is an optimist and a photographer. www.gilesgodwin.com

PAUL HAMILTON is now a happily married man according to his wife. No, he does not have a website

STEPHAN HARDING is resident ecologist at Schumacher College, Dartington and is the author of *Animate Earth* (Green Books)

ANTHONY HAYTHORNTHWAITE is an illustrator for hire, to contact him email anthony @aqhthestudio.co.uk

TONY HUSBAND is an award winning cartoonist who works for the *Times*, the *Express*, the *Sun*, *Private Eye* and many many more. For more information visit tonyhusband.co.uk

FANNY JOHNSTONE is a journalist who writes about the beauty, excitement and culture of motoring and whatever

else takes her fancy

DAN KIERAN edited *Crap Towns*, *Crap Jobs* and *Crap Holidays*. His book *The Myway Code* , co-written with Ian Vince, is out now, and his *I Fought The Law* comes out next year on Transworld

CHLOE KING is an illustrator. Her website is at chloeking.co.uk and she can be reached at chloeking@f2s.com.

PETE LOVEDAY created the legendary Russell comics.

MARK MANNING is sometimes Zodiac Mindwarp

JOHN MARCHANT, after ten years working in the New York art world, is currently on sabbatical and having an extremely nice time, thank you

JOHN MICHELL is a radical traditionalist. He is the author of many books and writes a monthly column in *The Oldie*

KEVIN PARR is a writer and angler. He recently became a white van man

ASH PROSSER is a poet living on his wits in Plymouth

GREG ROWLAND is a legitimate businessman

GWYN VAUGHN ROBERTS

IDLERS AT WORK; FROM LEFT, DAN KIERAN, GAVIN PRETOR-PINNEY,
CLARE POLLARD AND TOM HODGKINSON

lives in Wales and can only produce work when his mental state is a fine balance of energy and misery

IAN VINCE is a left-handed, Mac-compatible, asthmatic comedy writer, clearly looking for some kind of niche market. His book *The Myway Code*, co-written with Dan Kieran, is out now. He runs socialscrutiny.org and trepanning.tv and writes for telly and print.

CHRIS WATSON has a new t-shirt label at www.tonuppress.com and his work can be seen at www.chris-watson.co.uk

ANKE WECKMANN is based in London. Website: www.Linotte.net
Email: Linotte77@hotmail.com

GED WELLS is Insane. See him at www.insane.org.uk

TONY WHITE is the Idler's Literary Editor. He's just co-edited (with Matt Thorne and Borivoj Radakovic) a new fiction anthology called *Croation Nights*, which is published by Serpent's Tail

CHRIS YATES is a legendary fisherman, photographer and master of idleness. His book *How To Fish*, (Hamish Hamilton), is out in November

NOTES FROM THE COUCH

JEFF HARRISON

THE IDLER'S DIARY

THE LATEST exciting development in the life of the Idler has been the formation of The Idler Ukulele Orchestra. Rehearsals have been taking place at the Three Kings pub in London's Clerkenwell, and our band will soon be playing gigs in pubs, clubs, town squares and village halls around the UK. Among the numbers we will play will be "I'm Only Sleeping" by The Beatles, "Sunny Afternoon" by The Kinks and "Rat Race" by the Specials. We may also introduce one or two Noel Coward songs for a gentlemanly feel. The ukulele revolution has started and all you need to join it is your own uke. Truly, the uke puts music in the hands of the people. Indeed, the editor of this magazine was seen in various Dean Street taverns singing his ale-fuelled heart out the night

THE IDLER UKULELE
ORCHESTRA'S FIRST
REHEARSAL. CLOCKWISE
FROM LEFT: TOM
HODGKINSON, GAVIN
PRETOR-PINNEY WITH
FLORA; PAUL HAMILTON;
LIZ PICKERING AND
JENNY BEAUMONT.

after one rehearsal. In this issue, you'll find our Ukulele Special, with all you need to know abut the history and culture of the uke, plus how to play it, and a chance to win your very own top model, worth the considerable sum of £85.

IDLER DEP ED DAN KIERAN

Dan has been attempting to get arrested as part of his upcoming book *I Fought The Law: The Search For Albion In Modern Britain*, which will be published by Bantam in March 2007. As the government has seen fit to ban any spontaneous demonstration within a kilometer of Parliament Dan has joined a bunch of peculiarly English eccentrics hellbent on breaking this totalitarian legislation. So far he has dressed up as a teddy bear as part of an illegal picnic in Parliament Square, organized a cricket match for the Ashes of the Magna Carta on St George's day (which was mentioned in Vanity Fair) and gone on

TODAY'S THE DAY THE TEDDY BEARS TRY TO GET NICKED

JEFF HARRISON

IDLER'S DIARY CONTINUTED

A NEW MEMBER...

such as Bert Jansch, Voice of the Seven Woods, Louis Eliot, Circulus, Shortwave Set and many more, all for free. Bill Drummond came down and performed with his people's choir, The17. Aah, memories of a free festival.

WE WERE badly knocked earlier this year by the unexpected death at 40 of the great free spirit, Jago Eliot, of the Eliot family in St Germans, Cornwall. A hugely gener-ous, big-hearted man, Jago had long supported the Idler and was always ring-ing up with crazy schemes. At his funeral, we were all amazed to see an upside-down rainbow hovering in the sky above the marquee, a giant multi-coloured smile beaming down on us all. Clearly his spirit lives on. But the man himself will be sorely missed. 🐚

a thirty five mile pilgrimage from Runnymeade to Down-ing Street with a hippy who burnt the Magna Carta in a Tony Blair mask as soon as they arrived. As yet his middle-class force field has managed to prevent any actual bird, but watch this space...

GAVIN PRETOR-PINNEY's Cloudspot-ter's Guide has turned into a best-seller and we salute Gav for his great achieve-ment. All hail Gav, master of the skies!

If any of you still have not done so, it is still not too late to join the Cloud Appre-ciation Society by going to www.cloudappreciationsoc iety.org.
Gav also has had reason to celebrate as his little daughter, Flora, was born earlier this year.

TO LYNTON in North Devon, for the 4th annual Lynton and Lynmouth Music Festival, into which the Idler had some input this year. We lounged by the sea and watched acts

JAGO ELIOT (1966–2006)

READERS' LETTERS

Dear idler,

I don't know about you, but I have often wondered who it was (or is) that says that life has to be the way it is. It certainly wasn't me, and if you're reading this, I'm guessing it wasn't you.

The problem here is one of liberty, as a society. We are constrained as a nation to conform to Pax Americana, or the Protestant work ethic. What we really need is to set our own rules, ones congruent with whom the British (or whoever) are. We need to have societal ownership of society's rules.

How can the body politic be free, and the members of it at liberty and happy, if the body is shackled by rules and ideas from abroad.

This didn't happen by accident or conquest however, we willingly accepted the burdens we have taken. We accepted them because we were told that our individual freedoms would be extended by allowing our selves to be homogenised to the globalisation model. We were told that by opening up our markets to freer trade we would have more choices, more freedom to choose. By trying to be competitive in the global marketplace we would be increasing our national wealth. By being self interested the 'invisible hand' of Adam Smith's classical economics would guide us to the best set up. Individual freedom and open markets are the answer, we were told. But do we really want to be able to choose between foreign goods and domestic ones, when the domestic were perfectly fine.

As an idle chap, I believe that we should stop aspiring to be Sir Alan Sugar, stop bringing our kids up telling them that they should want to go to university and then go on to work in big business. Perhaps they would want to anyway. But maybe if we brought them up to want to work to improve the world they lived in, they would want to be farmers, plumbers, or carpenters.

If we patronise those who work for the good of this country, the farmers who work progressively (whatever your idea of progressive is, be it organic, less intensive, more environmentally friendly), the local carpenters and cabinet makers, rather than the multilaterals like Ikea, we will become more independent and stand a better chance of creating a society that more of us think is fair and free.

We might decide that growing our own vegetables or fruit is in the best interest of society, as most of us have gardens, and if Dave at the end of the road grows nice apples, and you grow brilliant potatoes, by eating your own, or trading with your neighbour, you will save money, 'food miles', and create a sense of community. We obviously can't force people to grow some of their own food, but if society decided that this was a 'good' perhaps we wouldn't need to.

Only by being truly free to decide can we ever really make the right decision. We must throw off the shackles of being stuck in an ideological rut; think change, and change will happen. So I urge you, from your armchairs arise, and help us become proud of ourselves, our nation, and most of all my potatoes!

We all have a duty to try and mould society into what we want, only then can we really enjoy the rights that a society provides – freedoms.

James Horsfall

Write to us at: **The Idler**, Studio 20, 24-28A
Hatton Wall, London EC1N 8JH or tom@idler.co.uk

DEAR IDLER,

Issue 37 of the Idler popped through the letterbox this morning. After a long stroll with the dog,a couple of cornbeef sandwiches... and various other non taxing jobs, I sat down with a cuppa and got stuck into this latest issue. I am and always shall be an idler and consider Tom's book *How to be Idle* to be *the* modern day bible. However, I, like the majority spend many a day in perpetual confusion from the moment of leaving the home or turning on the dreaded TV or picking up a paper or mag... at external forces beyond my control.

We all need consistency or mild routine of some form or other. I would therefore draw your attention to two minor details. In your Editors letter you quote Bertrand Russell: "Two hours with any child is enough for any adult". And then in the article entitled "School's out" I read with absolute horror that school is not compulsory for the little shits!

I myself have a seven year old and the very thought of spending every hour of every day with the shrimp utterly abhorrent (and yes I do love him with every fibre in my body).

Yours in confusion.
Conor Whitworth
Nottingham

DEAR IDLER,

With symbolic if none too subtle timing, my first copy of the *Idler*, a gift from my girlfriend at the time, arrived in the post on the day I handed in my notice as the editor of an entertainments magazine down in sunny Brighton.

After three years of never-ending deadlines, it had already been my intention to pursue an unashamedly slack regime as a freelance writer, broadcaster and musician—this is Brighton, after all—and I warmly embraced the book's defence of dawdling as legitimate full-time pursuit.

In the subsequent six months, I thought I was adhering to the magazine's basic tenets with a reasonable degree of success (lie-ins, seeing the sun for longer than a lunch-break, gin and tonics at inappropriate times and so on). Yet it was only the other day that it hit me: by Jove, I've got it! After half a year playing at being an idler, I'd suddenly nailed it.

The decision that triggered this momentous realisation may, admittedly, lack a little in terms of drama: quite simply, I'd been cycling into town for a work meeting and had signalled a right turn when I knew full well that my destination lay well and truly to the left.

To the right lay the sea. And despite the innumerable inadequacies of our seafront cycle path, the chance of a few minutes of salt air and sea view suddenly seemed like an offer no sane person could refuse.

Yes, it would take longer, and I did, indeed, arrive late. Yet not only was this a more than worthwhile pay-off for the pleasures of the journey, but it also ensured that I arrived in a correspondingly jolly frame of mind, making the meeting noticeably more enjoyable.

Since it was the sea that drew me, I propose an aquatic moral to this humble tale: that my right turn represented a step towards the thinking of a river, which knows there is no hurry—we shall get there some day. Thanks, Winnnie The Pooh, for that. Here's to meandering.
Marcus Odair
Brighton 🌀

SKIVERS AND
HEROES AND VILLAINS

IVOR CUTLER

The great Scottish poet died on 3 March of this year. Take a look at www.ivorcutler.org and remind yourself of his genius.

NAUGHTY FRIDAYS

When the *Daily Mirror* ran their exposé of former scouse poet Craig Charles and his alleged habit of taking incessant hits of crack while poring over pornography in the back of a car, it alleged that Charles describes these sessions as his "naughty Fridays". The mind boggles at what his Silly Saturdays and Mischievous Mondays may involve.

THE SHED

Notice reaches us of a charming magazine called The Shed, all about sheds. We love sheds because they are zones of liberty, pootling and dawdling, particularly for grumpy male idlers. So we salute this brave publishing venture. For your own copy, email alex@splashmedia.co.uk.

SYD BARRETT

Before the acid kicked in, Syd Barrett's Pink Floyd songs painted an English countryside blooming with whimsy, where Emily can play forever. He extols the pleasures of "lazing in the foggy dew, sitting on a unicorn" and "watching buttercups cup the light" ("Flaming"), and of the gnome who lay "amidst the grass, fresh air at last" and exhorted us to "look at the sky, look at the river, isn't it good?". "Bike" hints disturbingly at the pressures of the material world (pets, possessions—"some fine, some cheap,

The Shed
Issue 5   July 2006
for people who work in sheds or shedlike atmospheres

Special green issue / Treesheds
Snacks / Weathervane / Temples

This issue is sponsored by:
Enterprise Nation

most of them are clockwork"). In his two post-Floyd car crash albums, Syd's Albion vision is blighted and diseased. Streams, skies and village greens are no longer a sanctuary. Barrett closes the city/country gap with the astonishing couplet: "In the sad town, cold iron hands clap the party of clowns outside/Rain falls in grey far away" ("Baby Lemonade"). But it is in the lovelorn "It Is Obvious" where he waxes his finest poetic vision of a poisoned landscape. The meaning of life, if there is one, is "written on the brambles". And here he reveals the eternal suffering of *all* things: "The velvet curtain of grey marked the blanket where sparrows play/And the trees are the waving corn stranded, my legs moved the last empty inches to you..." Fanatics mourned the 36 year silence of Syd but, really, was there anything else that he needed to say?

STRIVERS
OF THE IDLE UNIVERSE

LAPTOPS

According to a recent survey, a huge proportion of office workers now work at home for two hours in addition to the hours they put in at the office. This tragic new development in the history of work is a result of digital technology. The laptop, which advertised itself as promising to free us from the office has in fact brought the office into our homes. Train journeys, which used to provide a delivious oasis of nodding off and staring out of the window, are now used for work. It is the same with all the other absurd and costly gadgets that are now on the market: they create more work and therefore idlers are getting very, very Luddite in their outlook. Throw off the digital shackles!

NADINE BAGGOTT

Ms Baggott is a "Celebrity Beauty Editor" who appears in Oil Of Ulay adverts, preaching the skin-improving qualities of pentapeptides. So incessant are her appearances that she has actually broken through the stupor with which we normally regarding cosmetic advertising

and their risible science. Two questions: doesn't her advocacy of one brand compromise the journalistic integrity of a "celebrity beauty editor"? And if we use Oil Of Ulay, will we too have a complexion of white rubber stretched over the mouth of a jam jar?

MYSPACE

Myspace is presented as revolutionary and as putting music in the hands of the people, but this Murdoch-owned website is actually a self-promotional car crash and about as revolutionary as Ginsters pasties. Yes, we know that it may have helped the great Lily Allen but Lily Allen would have made it without Myspace. Myspace was simply lucky to have Lily Allen, not the other way round. ◉

TONY HUSBAND'S JOKES PAGE

KNOWN TO HIS FRIENDS AS THE WORLD'S WORST JOKE TELLER, TONY HUSBAND ASKS A FEW FAMOUS FACES FOR THEIR FAVOURITE GAGS.

Tony Husband

A biologist is talking to friends about his research findings. "Some whales can communicate with each other at a distance of 300 miles," he said. "What would one whale say to another over 300 miles?" a friend said. "Im not totally sure," said the biologist, "but it sounds like 'Can you hear me now?'"

Gavin Pretor-Pinney

A woman is visiting a stately home. She is shown around by the guide. The woman says to the guide, "are there any ghosts here, because I'm absolutely petrified of them." The guide turns to the woman and says "I've not seen one since I worked here." The woman says, "how long have you worked here?" The guide replies, "400 years."

Tom Hodgkinson

What's a plumber's favourite food? A leek.

Rory McGrath

In the middle of the night, a guy goes downstairs and finds his grandad sat at the kitchen table. He says, "Grandad, what are you doing?" Grandad says, I'm trying to do this fucking jigsaw of this hen." The guy says, "Put the cornflakes back in the packet and go to bed."

Chris Yates

Two men go fishing and stay in a luxury hotel. And hire a sea cruiser for a week. They have no luck at all until the very last day when they catch a very small fish. On the drive home both me are depressed and one man klooks at the fish, do you realise this fish has cost us two thousand pounds? And the other man says, well thank God we didn't catch two then.

Griff Rhys Jones

My mate's spectacle are so thick if you look at an A to Z you can see people waving at you.

Terry Jones

An Englishman, an Irishman, a Welshman and a Soctsman are in a bar. The Engluishman says, "it's St George's Day today. My son was born on St George's Day and we called him George." The Scotsman says, "that's strange. My son was born on St Andrew's day and we called him Andrew." The Welshman says, "wow. My son was born on St David's day and we called him David." The Irishman says, "well my son Pancake..."

THE FINE LINE BETWEEN

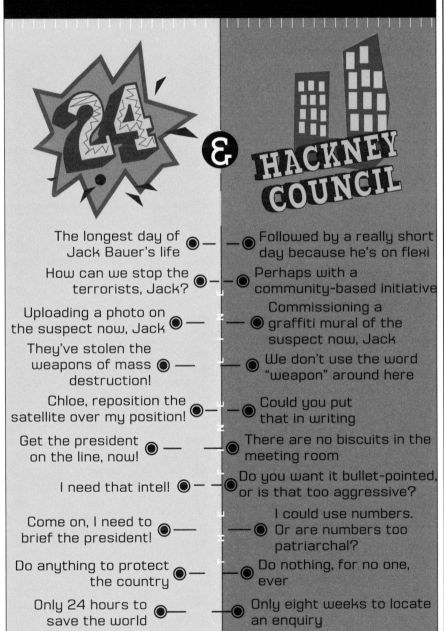

24 & HACKNEY COUNCIL

The longest day of Jack Bauer's life	Followed by a really short day because he's on flexi
How can we stop the terrorists, Jack?	Perhaps with a community-based initiative
Uploading a photo on the suspect now, Jack	Commissioning a graffiti mural of the suspect now, Jack
They've stolen the weapons of mass destruction!	We don't use the word "weapon" around here
Chloe, reposition the satellite over my position!	Could you put that in writing
Get the president on the line, now!	There are no biscuits in the meeting room
I need that intel!	Do you want it bullet-pointed, or is that too aggressive?
Come on, I need to brief the president!	I could use numbers. Or are numbers too patriarchal?
Do anything to protect the country	Do nothing, for no one, ever
Only 24 hours to save the world	Only eight weeks to locate an enquiry

THE FINE LINE

SCRAP TOWNS

Bristol's scrapstore offers a haven for junk junkies, says Adam Armfield

The Scrapstore has been a Bristol landmark for around 25 years. Schools, colleges and community groups come here to get their fill of materials discarded by industry, to use for both art and play. I went to look round, and had a chat with Jenn and Ellie (who work there), to see what it's all about. This is what they had to say:

"We're very keen on promoting recycling and creative play. We take waste from anyone, as long as it's safe and suitable".

"The items we have in stock change daily, it's very unpredictable, and we're gaining suppliers all the time. Lately we've had paint, tiles and fake foliage, along with the totally unexpected".

"The weirdest stuff is usually amongst the domestic waste, jewellery and old typewriters spring to mind. We had some latex body parts come in once. They were pretty disturbing, but people still took them".

Another Scrapstore one-off I remember was a box full of books entitled *Sheltie In Danger*.

Sheltie was a Shetland pony who went on adventures. She might have rescued people from mine shafts. There are a whole series of Sheltie books (at least 24 according to Amazon), including *Sheltie und der Doppelgänger*, *Sheltie, schnell wie der Wind*, and *Sheltie and the Saddle Mystery*.

A couple of years ago, the Scrapstore moved from central Bristol to their current location, an industrial building on the north side of town. "It's harder on the students now, they can't haul their scrap on foot so easily, but we reckon it gives them a chance to burn off all that booze".

"The Scrapstore owns this building, we rent out downstairs to the Better Food Company [an organic supermarket], and White Design [architects who design environmentally sensitive buildings]. Upstairs there are offices housing similar charities to us".

"We also do roadshows, taking a vanload of scrap to village halls outside Bristol and setting up for the day".

"It's pretty quiet in here when the sun's shining, but we get totally mobbed on rainy days".

There are scrapstores all over the country, they are independent but swap interesting stuff from time to time. They welcome donations. So, if there's a build up of waste at your company, give them a call, and get rid of some clutter. ◉

www.childrensscrapstore.co.uk

CRAP OR SCRAP? A FEW OF
THE DELIGHTS ON OFFER AT
BRISTOL'S SCRAPSTORE

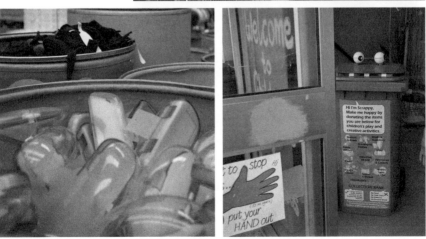

THE WIT AND WISDOM OF
AVA GARDNER

Collected by Rachael Field

The most glamorous star of 1940s and 50s Hollywood was under no illusions about herself. She made lots of risibly exotic pot-boiler flicks, most forgotten now (although her insouciant brand of singularly dotty brilliance lights up *The Barefoot Contessa*, *Night Of The Iguana* and *Bhowani Junction*). Acting was a method of financing her favoured lifestyle - a wild whirl of drink-crazed madness and a permanently revolving door of lovers, including Frank Sinatra, Sammy Davis Jr., Howard Hughes, Mickey Rooney and a few bullfighters. Ava Gardner was a very naughty girl and seemed to enjoy every debauched moment. So roll over Courtney Love and tell Paris Hilton the news...

AVA ON AVA

I'm a plain simple girl off the farm, and I've never pretended to be anything else.

Jeez, from the way people went on so, I thought I was better-looking than that...

I must have a Dr. Jekyll and Mr. Hyde split personality because I photograph so differently from my real character. Men seem to expect to see the femme-fatale sultry Jezebel dripping orchids and mink. When they see, instead, a skirt, sweater and saddle-shoe girl, with no make-up, it's a great let-down.

I know that keeping the lips slightly parted and wetting them occasionally with the tongue makes them appear fresh and appealing. So I do it.

HOT LIPS

People think I am the type who would take the busboy out back. And I just might.

AVA ON FILMS

I can't act! I can't do this fucking thing!

At thirty-two, I'm the second oldest actress at MGM. At the studio they call me "Mother Gardner".

Create? I don't create anything. I leave that to the scriptwriter and the director. I'm not an actress. I have no theories

Yes, I'm very beautiful. But morally I stink

about the job. I just do what it tells me to do in the script. I read it through and usually it is a terrible chore, the same old clichés over and over again.

....

I make films for the money. I owe my success to luck.

....

Being a star is a responsibility. It means I have to go forward or go back; I can't stand still. Sometimes I shiver and shake at the idea. Me. Who never had a nerve in her body!

What puckers my alabaster brow is whether or not I'll keep up full steam ahead or revert to type. As I said, I'm an old-fashioned girl. Hoot all you like, but what I really want is a home and kids. I'm not completely sure yet whether I'm going to be Forever Ambitious or not. One thing is a cinch, though. I won't be Forever Promising anymore!

....

The trouble was that I was a victim of image. Because I was promoted as a sort of siren, and played all those sexy broads, people made the mistake of thinking I was like that off screen.

....

Lady, if you happen to know anybody who could use a has-been actress with a wasted arm, a drooping lip, and reconstructed Southern accent, then I'm their gal!

AVA ON LOVE

....

I don't trust love anymore; it has led me astray.

....

AVA GARDNER CONTINUTED

AVA WITH HER BELOVED PAPARAZZI-BITING DOG, CARA

saying it's his turn to marry her:
Your turn? Howard... honey... you crack me up. You make it sound like I'm a pony ride at the country fair.

. . . .

To unidentified pompous English Actor:
Do you eat pussy?

. . . .

Frank Sinatra:
We became lovers forever-eternally...I truly felt that no matter what happened we would always be in love.

. . . .

(To Sinatra, in early-50s career slump:) No one with your talent is ever washed up. This is just a bad time. Here, rub my ass. It'll give you good luck.

. . . .

Reporter: What do you see in that 119 pound has-been?
Ava: Well, I'll tell you–nineteen pounds is cock. Honey, Frankie and I are both high-strung people. We explode fast, maybe faster than most married couples. But it's great fun making up.

. . . .

. . . .

To Howard Hughes:
I won't be fucking spied on! I'm not your goddamn property, you son-of-a-bitch.

. . . .

After she and Sinatra divorce, Hughes approaches Ava,

(To Grace Kelly:) Gracie, have you ever seen a black cock? (Lifting an African tribesman's loincloth to show her one.) Frank's is bigger.

Walter Chiari:
Walter was nice. [But the] distance that separates liking from love is as wide as the Pacific.

HOLLYWOOD COLLEAGUES

On Kathryn Grayson:
Graycie had the biggest boobs in Hollywood... with her they didn't need 3-D

On Clark Gable:
Clark is the sort of guy that if you say, "Hiya Clark, how are you?" he's stuck for an answer.

John Ford:
The meanest man on earth. Thoroughly evil. Adored him!

On swimming star Esther Williams:
A party isn't a party without a drunken bitch lying in a pool of tears.

On poet Robert Graves:
It was a love-conspiracy between us... Being with him and his wonderful wife, Beryl, and the kids gave me a kind of pleasure and satisfaction nothing else in my life could approach.

On Paul Newman:
One of my unfavourite actors.

On Charlton Heston:
Well, he wears a wig.

On Mia Farrow, a later Mrs Sinatra:
A fag with a pussy. I always knew Frank wanted to go to bed with a boy.

AVA THE GLOBETROTTER

Tokyo:
Hell! It looks like North Carolina, I hate this place already!

Spain:
I want a place right outside Madrid. If I don't find the right place I'll build something. My new contract says I make two films a year. Some of them may be a piece of cheese, I don't have the right to approve scripts in advance, and if some of them are made in Hollywood I'll go there, but home will be Spain.

You need to get the fuck out of Spain, because the guys all have little dicks and they'll fuck you in the ass before you can get your panties off. ☺

From the wonderful new biography, Ava Gardner, by Lee Server, Bloomsbury, £20.

WILD THINGS

Simon Prosser **on the noble weed**

What is a weed? I wondered as I thought about the work of the artist Jacques Nimki, whose recent show at The Approach Gallery in London included not only a series of drawings and collages of weeds (he calls them "florilegiums"—flower books) but also a real-life carpet, grown in situ, completely covering the gallery floor and smelling gorgeously peaty - a pastoral subversion of the boring white cube.

In search of an answer, I asked *Idler* gardening contributor, Tim Richardson. There was no strict definition, he told me. A weed is simply "a plant in the wrong place".

The weed is the underdog of the plant world, rejected by horticulturalists, yet gloriously tenacious (or what a gardener might call "invasive"). And that is what gives weeds their nobility. As I write there is one growing out of the urban soot in the gutter outside my window. How is it possible not to admire such determination?

From an aesthetic point of view there is nothing to distinguish a weed from a cultivated plant. Both are capable of great beauty. One only has to think of motorway verges, which frequently enchant with drifts of spring-flowering weeds. They are also, often, of medicinal and culinary value, as anyone who has cured a nettle-sting with a dock leaf, or eaten a dandelion leaf salad, will tell you.

In immortalising the weeds he finds on our city streets, Jacques Nimki makes us look anew at these misunderstood plants, and helps us to see in them virtues we should value - and even nurture in ourselves. 🐚

JACQUES NIMKI'S FLOWERY MEAD AT THE APPROACH GALLER

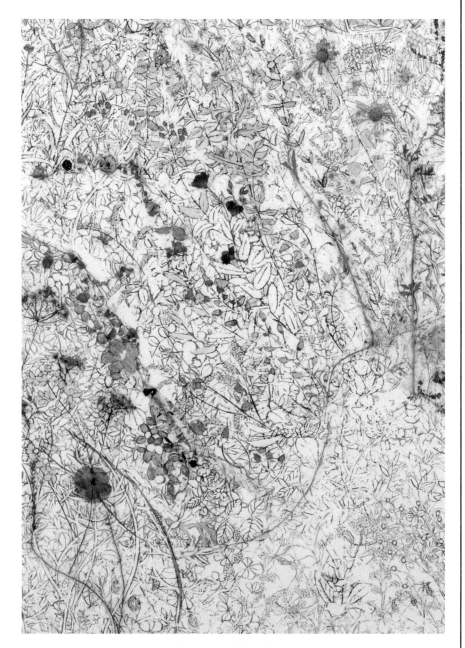

FLORILEGIUM (MARCH), 2006
ACRYLIC AND PRESSED FLOWERS ON LAMINATED BOARD IN OAK TRAY FRAME
202X139.5 CM

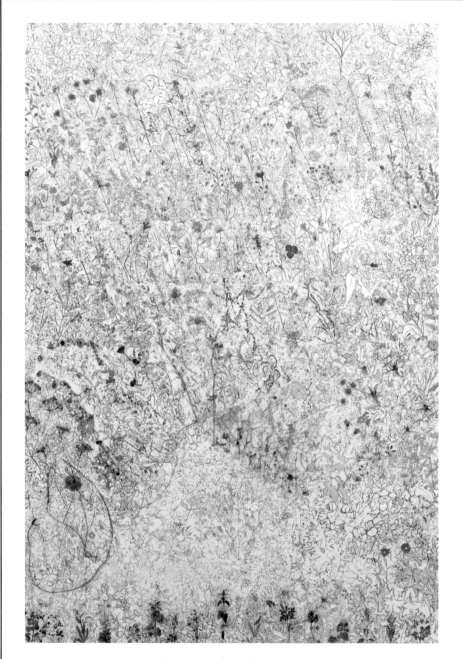

FLORILEGIUM (MARCH), 2006
ACRYLIC AND PRESSED FLOWERS ON LAMINATED BOARD IN OAK TRAY FRAME
202X139.5 CM

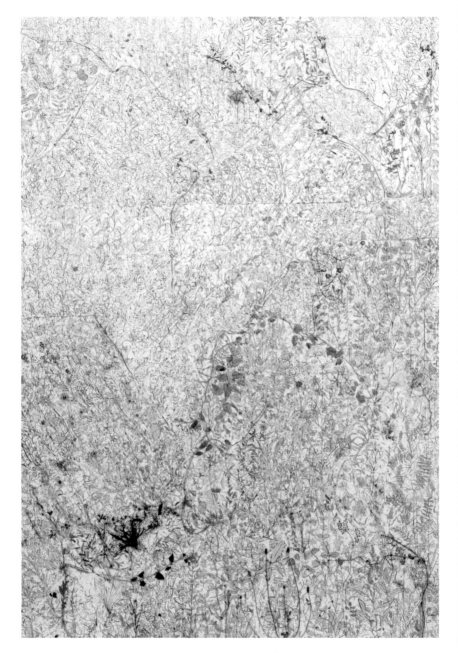

FLORILEGIUM (FEBRUARY), 2006
ACRYLIC AND PRESSED FLOWERS ON LAMINATED BOARD IN OAK TRAY FRAME
202X139.5 CM

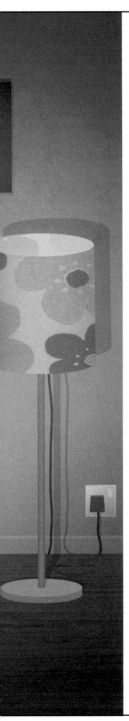

NATHAN FLETCHER

SWITCH OFF

Nick Kettles rediscovers the still quiet of the evening hour

After 25 years, we have finally taken the advice offered to my partner and I as children, by the theme tune to 70s and 80s school holiday listings-filler *Why Don't You?* – the kids programme which wittily invited viewers to switch off their TV set to go and do something infinitely less boring instead.

In fact we have done more than that. We have tuned out its ability to receive a signal and informed the TV License Authority as a spur to maintain our most holy vow of cultural abstinence.

At first giving up TV was not an easy task. It was a willing and versatile babysitter to our three and 18 months old daughters. We are not alone in this. According to research from Sheffield University 2000 parents of young children were found to be overwhelmingly positive about the role of TV in their children's lives. One in ten children knew how to turn on the TV and five per cent how to use a remote control before their first birthday.

Indeed, we know that TV can be a comforting salve to the responsibility of parenthood too. Soaking in the warm soapy suds of *Eastenders* or *Coronation Street*, with tea and toast, our money worries melted away, albeit momentarily. Taking the piss out of Big Brother contestants was like popping bubble wrap; the self-referential kind found surrounding members of the celebrity nation.

But the results of accommodating this cuckoo in our nest were starting to pile up.

Our younger daughter's eyes became glazed and spine slumped after just 15 minutes watching. Then there were the

I CALCULATED
THAT ANNUALLY
WE WERE SPENDING
A WHOPPING 52
HOURS DISTRACTED
FROM THINGS THAT
MIGHT ENRICH OUR
LIVES

tantrums that often followed switching it off. The way brand names like McDonalds and Barbie, somehow seeped into our daughters consciousness in spite of rarely watching commercial TV. The way TV became a subject of conversation with other parents at their kindergarten: "did you see Peppa Pig this morning? Wasn't it droll." Then the trip to Stoke on Trent theatre to see my eldest daughter's Channel 5 antipodean heros—dance troop High 5—live. At the back end of a fifty date tour, their fatigued bodies hammered through their routines, with all the spontaneity of a brick. Without the magnifying glow of the TV screen, they seemed, well, human, and my daughter knew it. She couldn't articulate it, but I could tell she was sensing the marketer's sophistry.

Exactly! How often have we been seduced into watching the next big soap revelation, the next big same relationship drama, the endless stream of bad news; in favour of reading say the Rohinton Mistry book given for Christ-

mas, writing my magnus opus, my partner learning how to use her new state-of-the-art digital camera, going to the pub together, cooking together, having a conversation for cripes sake!

We tried a few times to hide the TV in the cupboard, but it would find its way out again, each time the pressure of child care got too much, or, we were seduced by the Guardian Guide's purple prose. Indeed, we had already reduced its size to a mere 12 inch screen. "Surely it's your spare set?" my sister's widescreen family said, when they came to visit.

But, then one day, the tipping point came. Idling at my desk, I worked out how much time we were devoting to the tube annually. Based on a conservative 10 hours a week, (the national average is 18 hours if your were wondering) I calculated that we were spending a whopping 520 hours, or just over 21 days, or three weeks, each, distracted from things that might otherwise enrich our lives. That amount of time was just too valuable to ignore.

It was time to be really honest with ourselves. Just how much of the TV we had been watching in the previous year had stayed with us for more than the time it takes to smoke a post coital cigarette? *The Office*, yes. Gail Tisley's Village People quip in *Coronation Street*. That too. And, Peter Kay revealing the vapid production values of the Jonathan Ross show. Twice. But nothing else. It was true, these moments had come too far and few between and ultimately only served to highlight the over-riding banality of what remained. Like a gold-panner the wait for other such moments of TV gold, was just too much. So it went, sans aerial, licence, and tuning button into the cupboard to be called on for the occasional video and no more.

There were a few tantrums that followed from the kids, but I was amazed to see just how quickly their natural instinct to play, so long suppressed by TV, re-surfaced. My partner and I had more arguments for a couple of weeks, while things that had been left unsaid in favour of the distraction of the TV were aired and spoken. But then, suddenly, I, we, felt as if a huge weight had been lifted.

How can I put this? Giving up TV is nothing short of the mental equivalent of colonic irrigation. It's as if you have been mentally constipated on a diet of banality, and then suddenly, the flotsam of junk TV floating on the surface of your mind is jettisoned back, to the ether from where it came. Flush, it's gone. It's liberating, truly liberating. And it is only then you realise just how much it had dulled your senses.

Being given 21 days a year to play with, and the mental acuity with which to enjoy it, was, is, like being a kid in an all-you-can-eat sweet shop. You don't know where to start. God, I even devoured Lynne Truss's *Eats, Shoots and Leaves*, with an unholy passion for punctuation, no man in his thirties should rightly have. More evenings just to chat or talk on the phone with relatives. More nights at the pub with friends, including the wonderful evening watching, Liverpool win the European Cup last year. TV, yes, but a shared experience with more than a 100 people.

It's been 18 months since that fateful day, and I can report that the mental environment is still a rich and fertile place. I have started Rohinton Mistry's *Fine Balance*, two screenplays, and read loads of books. My partner has immersed herself in digital photography and as a result won her first contract. We've been to the cinema frequently. We've made five year plans together, caught up on paperwork. Conceived ideas for many many businesses which we may or may not fulfil. We have stayed up late preparing crafts for the children to make, or planning how to spend festivals like Halloween at home. I have read the newspaper reports I want to read, rather than have them selected by news programme researchers at the 10 o'clock news. Boy, sometimes I even take a couple of weeks off, and consumed no news at all confident in the knowledge that when I next look, humanity

will still be struggling with the prospect of facing extinction in the next 50 years.

But most of all I have re-discovered the still quiet of the evening hour. Freed from monotonous stream of broadcast talking heads, the acoustic environment in our home is alive. While immersed in a much loved book I can hear my breath rise and fall, the owl call, the bats squeak, a stray dog howling, a car roll pass the front of the house, the wind in the trees.

I would warn that anyone considering a similar move, should be prepared to be met with shock and amusement by friends and family. You will be a social lepers in their eyes, until that is, your life becomes so rich with new pursuits in your 21 days+ per year, that you won't give a shit what they think. Indeed, the longer you abstain the more you will wonder why you didn't do it earlier.

Yes, you may sense just a little conversionary zeal here, but you must understand that the template of my imagination has been expunged of the input of ubiquitous celeb faces such as Carole Smiley, Alan Titchmarsh, and the Jamie Olivers of this world. It is my duty to share the good news.

In a life of four score years or more, the average Briton watches TV for about eight years—just how much was essential viewing? 🌀

CLOUDED VISIONS

Clouds are the Rorschach images in the sky. Gavin Pretor-Pinney selects some of the best cloud lookalike photographs sent in by members of, and visitors to, The Cloud Appreication Society.

A BEAR, TRAINED IN THE CRUEL SPORT OF DUCK JUGGLING (ALSO KNOWN AS CUMULUS CONGESTUS)
SENT IN BY SENA ZUTIC

PEGASUS (ALSO KNOWN AS ALTOCUMULUS LENTICULARIS)
SENT IN BY NEVILLE SHULMAN

A WITCH ON A BROOMSTICK (ALSO KNOWN AS CIRRUS & CIRROSTRATUS)
SENT IN BY FRODE SVINTERUD

THE USS ENTERPRISE (ALSO KNOWN AS ALTOCUMULUS LENTICULARIS)
SENT IN BY AIDAN MCKEOWN

TWO CATS DANCING THE SALSA (ALSO KNOWN AS CUMULUS)
SENT IN BY MIKE RUBIN

THE GRIM REAPER (ALSO KNOWN AS STRATOCUMULUS)
SENT IN BY RICHARD UNWIN

THE FIRST KISS IS RUINED BY ONE PERSON INSISTING ON HAVING A FAG AT THE SAME TIME (ALSO
KNOWN AS CUMULUS AND CIRROSTRATUS) SENT IN BY SAMANTHA HALL

THOUGH YOU COME WITH SAWS AND AXES YET IN THE END I SHALL GROW OVER YOUR GRAVES

THAT'S JUST THE WAY IT IS

SUMMER SPORTS REPORT

Idler sports editor John Moore has filed his first ever report

JOHN MOORE, IDLER SPORTS EDITOR

THE WORLD CUP: When is it?

THE CRICKET: Disappointing

ROYAL ASCOT: Fragrant

WIMBLEDON: Rubbish

About Your Majesty, Ma'am

- For the purposes of Royal Protocol, this form may be completed on behalf of One by One's Serf or Brown Nosing Lickspittle, Gawd bless you, Ma'am.

- If it would please Your Majesty, please do not staple any dead pheasants to this form.

- Completion of this document entitles the Majestic Applicant to 1 (one) Pointlessly Glorious and Gloriously Pointless State Jolly.

- Once completed, this form will withdraw from Your Majesty's presence backwards and face down to the strains of a popular Beatles song made dreary and unnecessarily pompous by the Band of the Royal Marines.

Your first twelve forenames

Previous surnames, aliases and false identities
Please list any names you were once known by
ie: Saxe-Coburg-Gotha, Huns on the Run, The Regal Bank Vole, etc.

Please use this box to paint your individual graffiti tag (watercolour or oils only, please)

Please plot your marital status on the dianacamillagram below:

Top Camilla
Deemed unconstitutional
Not Safe For Church
Harmonious, yet somehow anodyne
Horsey society girl / professional bachelor
Wedding forms part of publicity brief
Doomed sham
Top Diana

Path of Charles

Partners over relative time and infidelity

IAN VINCE

National Identity Card Application Form

• Upon completion – and after the National Anthem has been dragged out for a mumble, like the tired old joke it is – if it pleases Your Majesty, One or a Member of One's Own Royal Gene Pool, may throw a bottle of fizzy wine against a sinister new government building, an anodyne memorial or a floating Death Machine of some kind.

BY APPOINTMENT TO HM THE QUEEN AND HER CONSORTIUM OF DULL, FECKLESS OAFS AND CHINLESS BUFFOONS. SUPPLIERS OF UNPARALLELED LUXURY AND A LIFE OF RILEY. APPARENTLY INFINITE TOLERANCE CO. OF GREAT BRITAIN.

Total number of imbecile children   One has a total of [ ] idiot spawn.

Items on One's Amazon Wish-List   [ ] Remaining third of Kent.

[ ] Gigantic fucking ship.

Serfs and nobs who work for One   [ ] Underlady of the Backstairs.

[ ] Lady Shaver of Gillette.

[ ] Tara Palmer Boom-de-ay.

[ ] Entire UK population.

Do you have any savings?   No [ ] Please see leaflet *About your girocheque.*

Yes [ ] Please communicate details of secret investments by mounting a co-ordinated cryptic display of half-mast flags, 21-gun salutes, One's Own motorcycle display team and Ascot head wear.

PRINTED BY THE HAPPY, COMPLIANT SERFS AT THE DEPARTMENT OF SOCIAL SCRUTINY – TO RE-ORDER, VISIT WWW.SOCIALSCRUTINY.ORG

IAN VINCE

IT'S MYWAY ON THE HIGHWAY

Ian Vince **and** *Dan Kieran* *show us a glimpse of their upcoming masterpiece, The Myway Code*

After 75 years of faithful service in the cause of road safety, with millions upon millions of copies sold, it's time for *The Highway Code* to get out from behind the wheel and take its place in the back seat, where its geriatric mutterings can safely be ignored.

In place of *The Highway Code* comes *The Myway Code: the Real Rules of the Road*.

The Myway Code is absolutely

essential reading for all Britain's road users. Written and laid out in a style which will be familiar to anyone who has seen, and therefore failed to read, the official Highway Code, *The Myway Code* puts its foot down and its finger up, as it rips up the L-plates and tears up the road like an XR3i full of feral children on alcopops. Motorists, cyclists and airline pilots must all take heed, as well as stupid horsey people and the scattered organs of crushed mammals.

Horse signals from the rear

I may or may not turn left or right at next junction and/or over the hedge. Who can tell?

The fly crawling up my back is about to make me bolt off, killing absolutely everyone concerned.

I am on a high-fibre diet and I will shortly be taking a long and satisfying dump on your car bonnet.

Warnings, orders and instructions

Saviour ahead

Anarchy

Cycle path mounted
on top of bus

Stuck-up Cassandras

Capture possible

Alien
cattle mutilation

You must not
deviate from
120 mph

Calamitous deviation over cliff

ON A GREEN NOTE
Dr Sleeves gets down

From Little Sparta to Prospect Cottage the spirit of the Green Man hovers through this scepter'd isle, manifesting in hedgerows, earthworks, pub signs and church carvings. Morris Men from Wilmington to Keswick invoke his presence and so can you with this Green Man jukebox: find these songs, slap an ASBO on yourself for the evening, dig out your clay pipe and tabard, turn the volume up and pour yourself a jug of Ole Spritely Magus. Are you ready? Then let's enter the floral dance of the mind.

1. Comus: A Song to Comus (1971)

This is one evil mother of a hoedown. The Green Man on a chthonic tip. Get yourself to Ludlow castle and hack back the years to 1634, when Milton's *Comus* was first performed in the hall on Michaelmas night. Whilst you're there, wander over to the churchyard to see where AE Housman's ashes were scattered and master the medieval energy of this Shropshire market town.

2. Sir John Betjeman: Indoor Games Near Newbury (1974)

"In among the silver birches, winding ways of tarmac wander," intones Betjeman at the start of this nostalgic paean to a time when the green lawns of Albion could coexist with the utopian dreams of the motor car. It's a far cry from Swampy. Imagine Tolkien's descriptions of the Shire crossed with Lancaster motorway service station and you're half way there.

3. Jethro Tull: Jack-In-The-Green (1977)

Taken from the mighty Tull's pastoral comedy album, *Songs From The Wood*, this will have you packing a flagon of mead and heading off to the nearest hedgerow to play the medieval game of "munting the pint". The English custom of binge drinking has its roots in this little known archaic and noble game.

4. Circulus: Miri It Is (2005)

Beyond Ludicrous. Drop some "Shropshire sunshine" and put this on repeat on your iPod for eight hours. I did just that in a field near Grinshill in North Shropshire last summer and returned to the Isle of Shrewsbury a changed man.

5. XTC: GreenMan (1999)

We're in Wiltshire now so how about a game of mangelwurzel hurling? That's if we can get hold of any of these scarce root vegetables. The game is like boules but played with a type of beetroot. After all, turnips and swedes are quite unsuitable for sporting purposes.

6. Roy Harper: New England (2000)

Tenantry Ground. Field System. Tumulus: I'm consulting OS Landranger 199 as I head out of Polegate on foot to see the Lanky Man of Wilmington. This is the perfect soundtrack for browsing in an army surplus store. I'm contemplating Blair's speed trap Britain and getting

AND DID THOSE FEET, IN ANCIENT TIME, REST UPON ENGLAND'S BENCHES GREEN?

tooled up with some cammo and woad. "Menace Geese To Be Culled" reads the headline of the local paper.

7. The Watersons: John Barleycorn (1965)

Lamb Ales, May Goslings, Kellums, Punkie Night and Crinkley Bottom. These are just a few of the customs that keep the Green Man manifested throughout the year, though obviously not in parts of the landscape that are ringfenced by signs which read: "Danger Area. MOD Ranges in the area. Danger! Observe Warning Notices".

8. Julian Cope: Lunatic and Fire-pistol (1983)

Ideal listening for getting lamped on pints of Shropshire Lad (2/3rd Guinness to 1/3rd Benylin Drowsy) whilst contemplating the monochromatic iridescent grey skies that define the depths of the English winter and the seething undercurrent of violence that make its market towns so distinctive.

9. Genesis: For Absent Friends (1973)

Whilst walking in Wilmington with Dr. Dodman, we came across the Green Man in the form of a bench in the local church (see photograph). He can be anywhere. It looks like you've just discovered the film in a waterlogged King George V biscuit tin that your Granny had and has only just had the film developed. A nice submerged codeine vibe.

10. The Waterboys: Universal Hall (2003)

One of the great modern travelogue songs, up there with Van Morrison's *Almost Independence Day*. From Taos Pueblo to Avebury, and Callanish to Cuzco. From Gallarus Oratory to San Francisco, or Dingle to Findhorn. From the dreamlines of the Olgas to the Chapel of the Holy Cross and on to Chaco Canyon, through North Shropshire and up to Grasmere. I'll meet you in Wordsworth's house and we can take it from there...

Dr. Sleeves is a reader in Green Field Thinking at the University of Clun in Shropshire.

FROM THE FORUM

Wit and wisdom and tips and tricks from the Idler's website

The *Idler* web forum is peopled by a lively bunch of reprobates, always ready to give advice on the idle life and swap stories about outfoxing authority or just funny things that have happened to them. We trawled through it to find a few choice snippets.

SARAH JANES ON PLAYING:

I think playing is good fun and I don't see why it should be the preserve of little kids. Adults should draw pictures and make music and get messy and sing songs and make things out of plasticine too. I think people who do these things are much happier than people who consider such frivolities silly. Also combining any of the above with having a drink is also EXCELLENT fun.

You know the other day when I thought my friends were marching their marching band in Mardi Gras, my friend Chris came over to my flat and we were going to do some band publicity work stuff. Instead we had a few white russians, painted ourselves special hats with the colours of mardi gras, purple, gold and green and draped ourselves in my collection of Mardi Gras beads, what I collected last year and listened to Al Hirt Dixieland jazz on my record player and danced a bit and then we had a Beatles medley jam, him on the guitar and me on my baby accordion.

He can play but I can't and we sung different Beatles songs at the same time and them some old classics like "Animal Fair" and "I stuck my finger in a woodpeckers hole" at the VERY top of our lungs and we laughed until we cried and then we walked around town in our Mardi Gras hats and beads and said happy Mardi Gras to everyone.

...AND MASTURBATING:

I was lying in bed listening to the radio in the morning a few months ago and they were playing some rousing classical music which made me feel passionate and sexy so there I am listening to classical music, masturbating, ready to climax and then they only go and start playing Elgar's Funeral March and I am caught wet and laughing between a rock and a hard place and can't come for toffee. Ahhhh!

SILMARILLION ON MAKING SOUP:

I love making home-made soup in the winter. My fave is really easy to make. chop a medium pumpkin up and boil it in veg stock for an hour. add some salt and pepper. After the hour, get a potato masher and mash the soup till smooth with a few lumps. Chop up a nice big bunch of fresh coriander (including the washed roots) and chuck it in. Cook it for another 10 mins. Then add half a can of coconut milk and a couple of chillies. Turn the heat right down so the soup simmers gently for about another 10 mins... then its ready. It can be frozen in person sized portions. Mmmmmmm very tasty

TERRY ON SAVING MONEY:

Don't pay for service contracts or warranties when you buy an appliance. You are protected by consumer laws.

Always buy trade paints when decorating your home. It's cheaper, goes further and applies easier.

If you live alone you should get 25% off your council tax bill.

Before paying for a prescription check what you're getting, some products are available without prescription and will be cheaper to buy.

Pay your credit card bill as soon as you get it. Your bill is monthly, your interest is not. Credit card bills again, always pay more than the minimum monthly payment, even if it's only a £1.

Frequently check the quantities of supermarket products. A common ruse is to keep the price the same and lower the quantity (200g becomes 175g, etc.)

If you fancy a flutter, the best prices available in the betting shop will be shown around 15 mins before the off. Never take the starting price.

LAGGER ADDS :

When shopping for an expensive item: leave the credit card at home, and don't bring enough cash to make the purchase.

Chances are you'll return home and rapidly lose interest shortly after.

SIR PERCY ON THE BEST EXCUSES FOR A SICKIE:

Ill-defined psychological maladies are by far the best tactic for controlling the DSS, albeit always make one of the ephemeral conditions a pronounced (if mercurial) agoraphobia. Every once in a while they will send you a "medical examination" threat but I have discovered a wonderful fact about these—if you ignore them they DO go away! The key is not to engage with the process at all even to the point of rehearsing tired excuses to them... do nothing whatsoever.

Never underestimate the great power and pleasure that resides in tearing up mail. DSS? Creditors? RIP and it's gone!

Oh, and re: the medical exam, it is actually illegal as a signatory nation to the UN charter to coerce people into medical examinations against their will. Which may be why they go away?

AND FROM TERRY:

Just turn up to work. Hang about for an hour (but this hour will be the best hour you've ever had at work, spend it relishing the moment) and then go and tell your supervisor/boss that you've just shit yourself.

Wait for a minute for it to sink in and say, "you understand that I'm telling you this in the strictest confidence."

Now he knows it's serious, say "obviously, I'll have to go home now," and walk out the door (affect a limp at your discretion).

If your supervisor/boss tells anyone, you're in for a treat—make a formal complaint and await your apology/cheque.

BRENDON ASKS:

Curiosity led me to write a simple spreadsheet to calculate how long I need to work to buy stuff.

For example, I would have to work for ten minutes to buy a take-away coffee from a franchise.

And I have to work for two hours and 39 minutes to earn the cost of getting to work.

QUERCUS ON LIFE IN THE CIVIL SERVICE:

I must admit this was a long time ago, when I "worked" for the big Customs Excise and VAT offices in Southend (one of several thousand employees spread amongst about 10 large office blocks in the town) and I was blatantly taking the piss out of the flexi-time system that operated.

The "core hours" were starting any hours between 7.30 to 9.30, lunch between 11.30 and 2.00, and finishing any time between 3.30 to 5.30, and you could go up to 11 hours either way in "credit" or "debit". I used regularly to turn up at 10, go to lunch at 11, come back (often pissed) at 2.30 and go home again at 3.30, and always had the full 11 hours "credit" on my timesheet.

I only ever got caught once in the seven years I worked there. The line manager told me he'd been taking a note of my arrival and departure times and would speak to me about my timesheet on the Monday morning. This was a Friday afternoon, and I was pretty worried all through the weekend as timesheet fiddling was a sackable offense. However when I arrived on the Monday morning it turned out he'd had a heart attack and died that weekend! Phew, that was a close one!

When I was actually at work my main activities seemed to consist of writing songs for the band I was in, using the photocopying facilites to print my fanzine and gig posters, and wandering off to other offices to idly chat up various office girls around the buildings that I fancied.

No one ever seemed to notice what I was doing, and I don't think I did a single stroke of actual work in the last two years that I was there. 🐌

Go to the idler forum at
www.idler.co.uk/forum

IDLE PLEASURES
STRAW SUCKING

As an aid to contemplation, turning a bit of grass around between your teeth has yet to be improved by anything the digital age can offer. Just pluck a piece of flowering grass from the meadow or from the wasteland by the train tracks, and chew and ponder. It's an instinctive pleasure, as ably demonstrated by Ermintrude in The Magic Roundabout. This simple act will instantly transform you into a Huckleberry Finnesque loafer, a Whitman, a Thoreau, drawing nutrients from the plant and enjoying the moment, free of the cares of the workaday world. Combine straw sucking with gazing off into the middle distance, shaking your head sagely and grinning with all the wisdom of a Taoist monk, and you may well be on the road to enlightenment. 🐌

GED WELLS

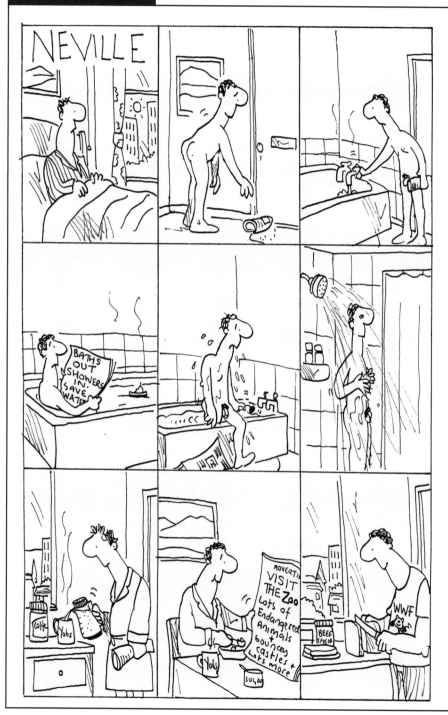

BILL AND ZED'S BAD ADVICE

WE'VE FUCKED UP OUR LIVES. NOW IT'S YOUR TURN

DEAR BAD ADVICE,

I have a character flaw I need help with. When I have friends over, after a few drinks, I like to play them records that I enjoy. The next day, their bored faces swim before my eyes but still, come midnight and a few units of alcohol, there I am at the stereo, presenting another song I love. Such enthusiasm is so unedifying in a grown man. How do you manage your impulses and enthusiasms? How do you suppress them?
Far Too Keen
Hastings

ZED: Excuse me, Mr Keen. Manage my impulses and enthusiasms? Suppress them? A life without rape, cannabalism and murder? Unthinkable dear boy, trés, trés unthinkable. If your grumpy, musically tasteless friends don't like listening to your collection of Death Metal and grindcore albums may I suggest you take a leaf out of my book and after you've raped and murdered them try sauteeing them with a few shallots a little salt, garlic and some fresh basil.
Bon appetit!

BILL: My dear Mr Keen

I am sure you won't mind me telling you that I'm currently on a fact-finding mission to Russia researching domestic violence in the post-Soviet era and to find what is the character flaw in Russian women that requires their menfolk to show them the back of their hand on 73% more occasions than the average British male needs to show his beloved the back of his hand. As yet my evidence is incomplete. As for you and your appalling taste in music I suggest you start importing some prime Russian progressive rock. Your friends will never want to leave. Lastly try dill as an alternative herb to the basil that Zed has recommended above. They use it a lot over her and it goes with most meats.

DEAR BAD ADVICE,

My wife is turned on by men fighting. When we go out, she is always trying to get me into fights, and a few times, she has succeeded. I am not that tasty and have been in casualty twice as a consequence. However, as much as I get hurt in these brawls, we do have amazing sex afterwards. Am I making a rod for my back by encouraging this kink?
Hurts So Good
Kentish Town

ZED: Dear Mr Good

Why not try combining the sex and the violence? When you're giving her a good seeing to why not beat the shit out of the mental pervert bitch at the same time. You never know, she sounds bonkers enough that she just might like it.

BILL: Are you sure your wife is not Russian? Moscow women seem to revel in watching all sorts of fighting and

violence. Every late-night bar I've visited over the past few nights has descended into communal fisticuffs. At some point in the proceedings womenfolk start to drag men from the melée and out of the bar. Naturally I thought this was to get them home and safely to bed. What I was later to witness in all the alcoves and doorways was copulating couples, with the sturdy Russian women taking the lead which seems to be the case over here.

.....

Hey Bill And Zed,

"If I am mental, am I allowed to kill someone and get away with it?"
A man posed this question to me the other day. He was smoking obsessively and his legs were agitated. To get myself out of the awkward situation, I promised to pass his inquiry onto you. Let me know your answer and I will forward it to him, next time he rears out of an alleyway, spitting alcoholic saliva at me.
MDA
Hackney

ZED: If you are the leader of a ruling political party, yes.

BILL: The short answer is yes. Kill them today. The slightly longer answer is, as I found to my regret, in Russia being locked up in the loony bin is pretty much the same as being sent to the Gulag for life. So if you're going to kill them don't come to Russia to do it. As for your agitated legs, try regular wanking, morning, noon and night. It deagitates the limbs.

Dear Bill And Zed

Could you see yourself getting behind David Cameron?
Guardian reader
Whitechapel

ZED: Only if he was stood at the top of a cliff.

BILL: Over here they have proper politicians. Could you imagine Putin riding a bike? When Putin needs to get to the airport, his cavalcade grinds all of Moscow's traffic to a halt, thus reminding the good Muscovites who is in charge. If your politicians are not in charge, what is the point of having them?

Ah, I just noticed you're from Whitechapel. Have you ever heard my theories on the Whitechapel murders. Invite me round for dinner when I get back from Russia. I will entertain you and your family with a full reenactment of the murders in your front room. One murder between each course. As for David Cameron, invite him round as well. He won't be riding that bike in too much of a hurry after that. And lastly, it has been brought to my attention by the internationally renowned Welsh artist Tracey Tracey that Russian men refuse to go down and chew the minge. Her theory is that that is why Russian women have such sour faces. If you have any thoughts that may throw light on this matter please contact me via the Idler. 🌀

CONVERSATIONS

In conversation with

Jamie Reid

JOHN MARCHANT **MEETS A VERY BRITISH ARTIST**

S
ome years ago, while living in New York, I was asked to collaborate with the artist Jamie Reid on a large survey of his work to date called *Peace Is Tough*. It soon became clear that his work ranged very widely indeed, from the endlessly reproduced and rehashed volley of cultural musket-fire with the Sex Pistols to contemplative watercolours which reflected his connection with the earth's subtler movements. At first there seemed to be stark contradictions here but as I started to look at the work and get to know Jamie it began to harmonize. In the intervening years, I've had the pleasure to get to know Jamie a little better. Spiritual descendent of post-Edwardian socialist reformer and Chief Druid George Watson MacGregor Reid, Jamie takes ancestral sighting points as disparate as William Blake, Gerrard Winstanley and the Diggers, Tom Paine, Wat Tyler and Simon de Montfort: in the words of Julian Cope, all "righteous, forward-thinking muthafuckers". There is, however, a smokescreen around him that veils his persona and work. He gets ignored by the art world for being unmalleable and gets pigeon-holed by an increasingly nostalgic press who only want to feed on the corpse of punk.

Born in 1947, Jamie Reid was a founding member of Croydon–based Situationist-inspired graphics unit Suburban Press and was responsible for graphics and layout for Christopher Gray's *Leaving the 20th Century*. In late 1975 Malcolm McLaren asked him to work with the Sex Pistols, providing both image and political agenda. Following their demise, Jamie drifted through places and projects—BowWowWow, Paris, performance work, the Brixton squat scene. In 1987 *Up They Rise: The Incomplete Works of Jamie Reid* was published by Faber and Faber. Co-produced with music journalist Jon Savage, it documented his influences and works to date. Reid got increasingly involved with various bands and protest movements: No Clause 28, the Legalise Cannabis Campaign, Reclain the Streets and Warchild to name a few. In 1989 he started a ten year commission to revisualise and reinvent the interior spaces of both the recording and resting spaces of the East London-based Strongroom Studios using "colour magic and sacred geometry" to encourage creativity and calm. He also spent five years as visual co-ordinator with the band Afro-Celt Sound System. He is currently finishing a heroically-proportioned 6-700 piece project based on the Druidic calender: "The Eightfold Year".*

We met east of Knighton, Powys, on the Welsh borders, at a spot fiercely contended in the wars with the English. It was here also in 1921 that the antiquarian photographer Alfred Watkins had a revelation about the hidden connections within the British landscape that he later wrote about in *The Old Straight Track*.

JAMIE SUBHEAD

"The root and inspiration and acknowledgement of the esoteric spirituality contained in the work comes from the ancient past and the distant future but is based in the immediate here and now.

It is indebted to those from the base root, the true guardians of the planet – the peasants.

Those of the earth
The rain and sun
The wind and stars
The seas the rivers
The valley the mountain tops
Mother Nature's citizens, those who tilled and toiled and understood the meaning of being.

Who loved the planet's smallest intimacies and its universal magnitude and used it for the good of all. The Mothers of Invention."

* *These are the eight festivals which divide the Wheel Of The Year. Each has its own Druidic celebration, with occurences approximately every six weeks. These include solstices, equinoxes, and the four major points in the turning of the Wheel, (Autumn, Winter, Spring, & Summer).*

NATURE STILL DRAWS A CROWD (1973) MIXED MEDIA COLLAGE, 297MM X 420MM

IDLER: Jamie, you spend a lot of time now with your hands in the soil. Can you tell me about that?

REID: [Takes out his trade tools and starts to paint] It is part and parcel... sowing, planting, growing, harvesting, nurturing. We are custodians of this planet... the Garden of Eden, paradise on earth. We have mostly done our best to fuck the planet up. My work is deeply affected by my time spent working the land. Organic growth is integral to it. I'll spend hours gardening and then go staight into hours of painting, they merge and intertwine with each other. It really is at the heart of my spiritual beliefs: love and respect for nature and our part within it.

IDLER: I think you still have to explain what you think a lot of your painting work is about, because people can't get their head around it.

REID: I read an awful lot of Jung when I was 17 to 19. That was the same time I was into RD Laing and David Cooper and all that. Funnily enough that was all around that squatting scene.

IDLER: And what about your belief system?

REID: Lapsed Druid! When you actually open things up to ordinary people – I mean ordinary people who would never fucking be bothered to go to an art gallery or museum – and I think quite rightly in lots of ways... I think magic has always existed to people of the land. They just knew–didn't need loads of mumbo jumbo ritual, they just knew... because they fucking looked. And we can't see anymore.

MONSTER ON THE ROOF (1974), WATERCOLOUR, 210MM X 297MM

IDLER: Alfred Watkins says that the people who laid out the Old Straight Tracks attained a supernatural aura because they had a knowledge that other people didn't. Isn't it natural for people to want someone to look up to?

REID: As soon as you get pyramidical hierarchies the whole thing becomes corrupt. We've never lived in an age where people trust each other less. I can remember in Croydon, specifically in the early 1970s when we were doing Suburban Press, which was far from being élitist and was very involved with the working class in that area–that was the first time ever we didn't have our doors open so it all started going then–but the whole Craig and Bentley thing really fucked Croydon. [The innocent and mentally ill Christopher Craig was hanged after his accomplice, the under-age Craig Bentley, killed PC Sidney Miles during a botched robbery in Croydon]. Then the police wouldn't go there. Croydon was very different then.

IDLER: Have you done any of your own research into ley-lines? What they are, what they mean?

REID: Only by observing and looking and seeing. A few years ago I was doing a lot of geometrical paintings. I tend to do them and then find the source. I knew about sacred geometry but it wasn't until I immersed myself in it that I realised what it was. In a way there was always that element of being self-taught. It's just such a fundamental element in everything–from primitive to the Renaissance to anything you care to name. You can see it reveal itself in front of your eyes in the landscape. You just immerse yourself in it–it's just a total experience where you completely lose yourself. It's the same as I feel when I'm actually working because I do go into a complete trance– which is why I can't talk and paint. It's very intense. It's very deep in.

IDLER: Were you ever a teenager?

REID: I can't remember! Maybe I've never stopped being one. I think music's probably the biggest influence, from early rock'n'roll. Croydon

"AS SOON AS YOU GET PYRAMIDICAL HIERARCHIES, THE WHOLE THING BECOMES CORRUPT. WE'VE NEVER LIVED IN AN AGE WHERE PEOPLE TRUST EACH OTHER LESS"

PEACE IS TOUGH (1991), MIXED MEDIA COLLAGE, 914MM X 609MM

was a really big centre of early Teddy Boys... and the whole Bill Haley thing had a massive effect. But I suppose more than anything the biggest influence was what was happening in jazz in America at the time.

IDLER: Where was it coming from? Through the radio or through friends?

REID: I was buying it as it was coming out. That would have been predominantly Mingus, Coltrane, Pharoah Sanders, Archie Shepp, Ornette Coleman. To me it was like a whole peak of 20th Century culture. It's never been surpassed. I also went to see a Pollock exhibition when I was about 16 without knowing anything about modern art and just found them like entering other worlds.

IDLER: You describe Pollock's work as being like landscape painting.

REID: It was just like fantasy worlds you could walk into and see what you liked. I loved the fact that they left themselves open to interpretation. And Blake. I was obsessed with the Blakes in the Tate. A lot of that I got through my father. There was always art and sport, and I was lucky enough to be really good at sport. As you know I was going to play professional football or cricket. I also used to go up to see Mingus and Sonny Rollins perform at Ronnie Scott's and Soho then was a big influence—at the same time Zappa, Beefheart and all that—it was an amazing period. There was a great element of experimentation. It was all part of a great belief in change, but I was brought up politically. My parents were diehard socialists and were very much involved—as was my brother—in the anti-war movement, so I was dragged off to Aldermaston marches at an early age.

IDLER: Your mother had problems with your Great Uncle George. She sounds like she was quite an iconoclast herself.

REID: She was brought up in a back-to-nature environment and her dad wrote a book called *In The Heart of Democracy* so they were all involved with the socialist movement of the time. It

"I WAS OBSESSED BY THE BLAKES IN THE TATE. A LOT OF THAT I GOT THROUGH MY FATHER... MY PARENTS WERE DIEHARD SOCIALISTS SO I GOT DRAGGED OFF TO ALDERMASTON MARCHES AT AN EARLY AGE"

"WE'VE BECOME MORE REPRESSED SINCE 1968. WE'VE BECOME MORE AND MORE UNDER THE THUMB. WE'VE LOST OUR BELIEF THAT PEOPLE CAN EFFECTIVELY CHANGE ANYTHING"

was the death of the whole fifty year epoch of Victorianism. There was a massive interest in change both politically and spiritually, which is the thing that fascinated me about the Druid order. There was a great belief in access to freedom of knowledge, education, the whole alternative movement in medicine and health, and health foods, but they were as likely to be on trade union and suffragette rallies as be doing rituals at Stonehenge. It was all part and parcel, which is something I've really tried to continue myself.

IDLER: Do you think this was a direct response to the Second World War?

REID: Well the war drew a curtain on everything. It was the most massive blood sacrifice in the history of mankind. I'll have to stop painting - I can't paint and talk at the same time.

IDLER: Rolf Harris can do it.

REID: He's better than me.

IDLER: 1968 was something of a watershed in the history of public protest—Paris burned in the belief that revolution was imminent, Martin Luther King was assassinated, the Tet Offensive began in Vietnam and medal winners Tommie Smith and John Carlos raised their fists for the Black Panther movement at the Mexico Olympics. What was your experience of London in 1968?

REID: It was part of that whole RD Laing and Cooper period. Everyone was looking for alternatives. It was a period of fantastic possibilities and change. People really believed that you could actually change things, and politically, things couldn't have become more repressed since then. We've become more and more under the thumb. We've lost our belief that people can effectively change anything. But on one level we're going through a period of the most massive change that we've ever been through in the history of woman or man-kind. There is a quickening process—we're experiencing everything that everyone's ever been through over millennia in one generation. I think America is Rome and it will fall very fast. On

EIGHTFOLD YEAR (2000), GOUACHE, 102MM X 152MM

STUDIO THREE – STRONGROOM STUDIOS (2000), MIXED MEDIA INSTALLATION
INCLUDING SCREENPRINT AND ACRYLICS

OVA (2000), GOUACHE, 6"X4"

an economic level it's going to China and India isn't it? I think everything might just break down. We'll go back into small states. China will break up, India will break up, everywhere will break up into smaller units because people can only really survive in smaller units. I think they can only really appreciate what a wonderful planet... God, I sound like Louis Armstrong! It's such a beautiful fucking place and we're the custodians of it and fucking economics... is Babylon. People could be very happy with fuck all.

IDLER: Is this what connects the dots in your work—your wish to make people think that they can really enjoy this world?

REID: To a great degree, yeah. I suppose on one level there is that element in a majority of my stuff which tends to be around painting or photography or bits of filming that I've done. There's an appreciation... a great element of beauty in it, just seeing the magnificence of things. And there's obviously that other element—the political element —the punk collage, punk, whatever you want to call it—agit-prop—which is making comment about the evilness of the powers that be. I don't see any contradiction in the two but it's something that I do suffer from as an artist, in terms of the people who run Culture. I don't fit into one category. I would've thought that the whole idea of an artist is to be expansive, like an explorer going forward. Not stuck in a rut. When it comes to a CV of exhibitions I've done, about a third of them aren't recorded. I did an exhibition with Ralph Rumney that I think Stewart Home organized. There was also a thing I did around the time of the first Gulf War which I did with John Michell in Camden, an exhibition about peace where he had all this sacred geometry stuff. If we're talking about influences John Michell is one. The man is like a modern day wizard. I love him because he's so benign. Such a lovely person.

IDLER: When did you first cross paths?

REID: Probably in the sixties, with the pamphlets

"IF WE'RE TALKING ABOUT INFLUENCES, JOHN MICHELL IS ONE. THE MAN IS LIKE A MODERN DAY WIZARD. I LOVE HIM BECAUSE HE'S SO BENIGN"

"ONE OF THE
THINGS I'VE
ALWAYS WANTED
TO DO IS TO
DO LANDSCAPE
SCULPTURE AND
CREATE GARDENS.
I'D LIKE TO CREATE
PLACES IN WHICH
PEOPLE CAN STAY
WHICH ACT AS
A RESOURCE"

he did on sacred geometry and ley-lines. Obviously there's the big connection from him to Watkins.

IDLER: So at last we get a mentor.

REID: A very gentle mentor.

IDLER: Where is he now?

REID: I think he still lives in Powis Square—I think he has done since the Sixties. In Notting Hill.

IDLER: You recently found out that MI6 had you down as a traitor.

REID: They were thinking of doing us for treason at the time of the Queen's jubilee and "God Save the Queen" and all that.

IDLER: Is that encouraging?

REID: I dunno. I think it's a family tradition. My brother was tried for treason when he was part of Spies For Peace and the Committee of One Hundred. See? Blame your parents!

IDLER: When you finish the Eightfold year cycle of work... what are you going to do next?

REID: I'd like to do more work like I did in the Strongroom. One of the things I've always wanted to do is to do landscape sculpture and create gardens. I spent five years doing landscape gardening when I was younger. I'd like to create places in which people can stay which act as resource centres. I'd like to apply what I've done in the Strongroom to all sorts of situations, it could be a hospital... obviously there's a whole element to what I do that has that capacity to heal people.

IDLER: Colour magic?

REID: Yeah. I don't think we know fuck all about colour and its potential. I don't think we know fuck all about sound. I think we're incredibly ignorant, however sophisticated we think our technology is. Actually, in a laborious way, technology hints at things we've lost the ability to see for ourselves. To me that was most well articulated by a Scottish engineer called Professor Alexander Thom who was a great expert on Stonehenge; he came to Stonehenge not through drugs or hippie-dom or New Age but through being an engineer and being

JUMP SHIP RAT (2002), LITHOGRAPHIC PRINT, 297MM X 420MM

GOD SAVE OUR YOBS (2006), MIXED MEDIA COLLAGE, 210MM X 297MM

fascinated with its structure. I remember him in a documentary–it was the time when Yale University had spent two years studying Stonehenge–saying "Oh yes, it's a cosmic timeclock". He was asked how on earth could these people could have built something like this without calculus? Fuck calculus. They were so in tune with the landscape, they were so in tune with the stars and their movements and the sun and the moon that they just knew. We had to spend thousand of years of calculus to come to these conclusions.

IDLER: I remember you saying that computers were going to bring in a whole age of...

REID: Backache and blindness.

IDLER: No, you said there would be a new age of psychic connection between people.

REID: I've probably got more cynical since I said that.

IDLER: The London Psychogeographical Association is about to post a section on their website about Druidry. What's the connection?

REID: I think we touched on it earlier when we talked about the whole period of say, the Golden Dawn and the early Druid Order in Britain–it was as much politically bound as spiritually bound–it was part and parcel of the same thing. If you look at the early trade union movement it was as much spiritual as it was political–but those things have become less and less apparent.

IDLER: Beuys used ritual as the kick-off point for a lot of his work which is now relics of his rituals. What comes first for you? Do you use artwork in rituals or does the work come from ritual?

REID: They are totally intertwined and totally interdependent. The whole process of how I work is very ritualistic anyway, in many ways. Setting up, starting and just doing it–it's very ritualistic –but I do go into a state of trance. You go into an absolute void–making your mind absolutely blank. Just letting it flow through.

IDLER: Do you have realizations in that state?

REID: Well, the realizations manifest themselves in what you do and what the product is. It's as much science as it is art. It goes into all sorts of situations. It's the high end of chemistry, physics, mathematics– things astrological. But you have to go through a deep sense of void and purity to do it. It's macrocosms, it's microcosms, but it's fundamentally there to make people feel uplifted. To make people feel good. Well, that side of my work is, but there is the other side–the overtly political side that's purely to make comment on how fucking evil the powers that be are.

IDLER: "Ne Travaillez Jamais"– please discuss!

REID: Well, our culture is geared towards enslavement, for people to perform pre-ordained functions, particularly in the workplace. I've always tried to encourage people to think about that and to do something about it. ☯

www.jamiereid.uk.net

RECOMMENDED READING

Up They Rise: The Incomplete Works of Jamie Reid by Jamie Reid and Jon Savage (Faber and Faber, 1987)

The Old Straight Track by Alfred Watkins (Abacus, 1974)

The Wing of Madness: The Life and Work of RD Laing by Daniel Burston (Harvard University Press, 1998)

FEATURES

To Sow a Meadow

WHEN RICHARD BENSON DECIDED TO SOW A WILD
FLOWER MEADOW, LITTLE DID HE KNOW WHAT
TRIALS LAY AHEAD

How's your meadow coming along?
You probably wouldn't imagine that any sentence of that length, let alone one that contains the word "meadow" and sounds like a olde-worlde hey-nonny folk song, could prompt unpleasant feelings in anyone. But it does in me. To me, this innocent, pastoral enquiry is like a nettle-and-thistle bouquet. When friends and strangers ask me this question–as they often do –I blush, rub the side of my neck, avert my eyes, mumble and, finally, tell lies.

"Fine!" I say. "We cut it back in the Spring, got rid of a lot of docks. When the ox-eye daisies came out at the end of June, it looked like a 1980s Timotei advert!" But although the daisies did grow, the truth is that they lasted about one week. The docks all grew back, stronger than before. My meadow is not fine at all–it is a small, green(ish) disaster area.

SLEF HEAL

The story of the meadow really goes back to my childhood, which I spent on my family's farm in Yorkshire. It was a small, crops-and-livestock, in-the-family-for-a-million-years-or-something farm, and as the eldest I should have taken it on, but as I was born with a Frank-Spencerish tendency to crash tractors and let animals escape, I was packed off to the city at 18. My younger brother stayed, but it got harder and harder to make money, and at the end of the 1990s they had to sell up –although, being luckier than most, they retained a bit of land with a shed beside a lane. I went back to help with the sale, and during that unsettling time I found myself somehow growing closer to my dad and brother than I had been before. Ours had not been an organic farm–indeed in the 1970s my dad was pulling out hedges and chucking pesticide on with all the gay abandon the Government was then encouraging with its intensifi-cation grants. However, what struck me when I went back were the practises which suddenly seemed terribly fashionable, but had always been followed because, not so very long ago at all, they just made good business sense. We fed the rotten potatoes and peelings to the pigs, the pigshit went on the fields, the fields grew more potatoes for us to eat. We butchered a pig and gave bits to neigh-bours, the neighbours gave us their spare garden fruit and veg. This wasn't in the pre-mechanisation era or anything, it was in the time of home com-puters, the Cold War and house music, and when I talked to my dad about it all in the weeks after the sale, I realised how much he knew about what are now called sustainable methods, and how his generation had been encouraged to abandon the knowledge in the rush to produce cheap food after the war.

It all got to me a bit, and that's how I decided to make a little wildflower meadow near that remain-

GROUNDSEL

MY PATCH OF GROUND WAS COVERED IN GOOSEGRASS, THISTLE, IRONWEED, GROUNDSEL AND DOCKS

ing shed. I wanted it to be a small, personal monument to a way of life that was disappearing, and I was determined to do it organically, so as to use the stuff my dad knew about pre-pesticide weed control.

This, of course, was my first mistake. I was drawing on a dodgy, modern, urban idea of "nature" rather than anything based on what might actually happen. The idea I mean is the one promulgated by some environmentalists and taken to heart by well-meaning urbanites, that vaguely suggests the earth, left to its own natural devices, will bring forth good things if you work "in harmony" with it. The trouble with this theory is that it ignores the fact that some plant species—generally inedible and unattractive ones—are, like some animals, aggressively predatorial. Sure, wild mushrooms or handsome foxgloves might flourish in undisturbed hedgerows, but once most ground has been disturbed in some way it's up for grabs, and only frequent human intervention will sort it out.

My patch of ground was covered in goosegrass, thistle, ironweed, groundsel and docks, all the nasty predatorial plants that take over this sort of soil like property developers taking over inner cities. I said I'd dig them out. My dad, as bemused as you would be if you'd spent your teens hoeing weeds in turnip fields only to have your aching back muscles saved by ICI's agri-chemicals, pointed out that it would be a lot easier to spray them off. I dug. It took a day to do about five square yards; in the end, he put a digger bucket on the front of a forklift and and scraped the top layer of soil off. I knew there would be weed-seeds left in there, but thought that a thick sowing of his meadow mixture would out-compete them.

When it came to choosing the seeds, I went to the seed merchant in the local market town to ask them to make up a mixture I had in mind. Unfortunately, the bloke explained, they didn't clean and mix their own seeds now; EU regulationss had made it too expensive, so now they just sold pre-packaged mixtures you from a global corporation whose HQ is in Canada. He gave me their glossy catalogue, which I took away and threw in the bin when I got home. In the end I found a wildflower farm near Nottingham, and began with a meadow mixture of standard proportions (80% grasses to 20% flowers), but using species that do well on chalky soil. Lots of wild flower species, such as ox-eye daisies, ragged robin and bird's foot trefoil, will grow almost anywhere, but many tend to thrive in certain conditions; woodland flowers like native bluebells, for example, seem to do better in acidy soils while those which like drier, well-drained soils (agrimony, for example) prefer chalk. The basic calcerous-soil mix had about five varieties of grass, and it is worth reciting their names: sheeps fescue, browntop bent, chewings fescue, creeping red fescue and crested dogtail. In addition to that there were about fifteen varieties of flower, including birdsfoot trefoil, corn poppy, cowslip, lady's bedstraw, salad burnet, self-heal, wild carrot, marjoram, musk mallow and meadow buttercup.

To this mix I added a selection of seeds bought separately. These were species likely to do OK, and that either were favourites of my family, or that had names I liked, such as

COLUMBINE

IF ANYTHING THERE WERE FEWER WILDFLOWERS THAN THERE HAD BEEN TO BEGIN WITH

speedwell, foxglove, and heartsease. The common names of wild flowers, with their rough lyricism and local variations seemed bound up with the sort of rural traditions that were worth keeping to me, so choosing them on this basis seemed to make some sort of sense.

When my dad and I sowed the mix of grass and wildflower seeds together later that day, at a rate of an ounce to every ten square yards, I imagined what it would all look like in eight months time. It felt to my naïve mind like a small, symbolic act of faith, continuity.

Of course, what it actually looked like in eight months time was a carpet of dull green and mustard-coloured groundsel with thistles and dock spears sticking up in it. If anything there were fewer wildflowers in it than there had been to begin with. The only positive point was that, bizarrely, a small clump of clover had flourished down one side, which would be good for the soil. Even my friend who worked in nature conservation told me to spray the weeds off this time, but I thought maybe if I dug down deeper this time it might help. I went to see my dad's friend Mal, a morose, bearded, heavy-browed stereotype of a Yorkshire farmer who I knew owned a mechanical garden rotavator. Mal and I had always got along quite well, because of—rather than despite—my lack of practical abilities. The misery that my clumsiness used to cause in me somehow chimed with the misery that life in general seemed to induce in Mal, so there was a kind of bond between us, although he had thought staying on at school at 16 had given me some funny ideas. He clearly saw my interest in the rotavator as being one of them.

"Is tha sure, lad?" he said, doubtfully, after showing me how it worked.

"I should be all right, shouldn't I?" I asked, unconvincingly. The rotavator was a lot heavier than I'd expected.

He just stared at me, quite kindly really, over his beard, and I said, "Are you worried I'll break it?"

"Nay!" he said. "I'm worried it'll break thee."

It was his pity that killed me. "This isn't going to work is it, Mal?"

In the end, he put a big, tractor-mounted rotavator on the back of his chunky International XL 955 and came up the lane to tackle it the modern way, with me on the footplate. "Why don't tha just get some Round Up on the bastard?" he said, sizing up the groundsel.

"I wanted to do it without sprays if I could, just, er, a thing, you know."

He looked at me in much the same way he looked at me 20 years ago when I said I was moving to London.

"Oh. So tha's one o' them, is tha?"

"I suppose so."

He didn't say anything.

"Can you try to go round that clover?" I asked meekly.

"Thee and thy bloody... *clover*," he said inexplicably, and lowered the spinning rotavator blades into the ground.

Naturally the weeds all choked the second lot of seed as well, and that autumn I put on a hand-pumped knapsack sprayer, and let the sticky, thorny, creeping vinous little bastards have it, full on. I felt like a rural version of Robert De Niro in *Taxi Driver*, and I understood in a new way what my dad had meant when he explained how the new pesticides had seemed

THISTLE

like miracles when they came in after the war. He'd be the first to acknowledge the damage they've done, by the way, but still, I suppose you have to realise that ideas that someone like me has about getting closer to nature are in some ways a product of the technology that distanced us from it in the first place. There is little enjoyment or dignity in hoeing weeds from ten acres of turnips if you have no other choice.

In the end I sprayed it twice, and that did tip the balance a bit. After the next lot of seed enough grasses came up to keep a lot of the docks and thistles back. You could even find the odd bit of speedwell and campion in there. By this time the book I'd written about my family and the farm had come out, and to my surprise my brother said that now he knew "what the fuck I was getting at with the flowers", he would help. He helped me mend an old lawnmower (by which I mean he did it while I passed him the spanners) and we mowed it together. Passers-by who'd read it would give me advice, although none of it worked except for the instruction to keep pulling the weeds out which was given to me by an agronomist who himself was cultivating a meadow in his paddock.

Every autumn and spring I and whoever else feels sorry for me will dig out patches of rubbish, and try to put down new seeds, or even transplant seedlings, and every summer a minuscule percentage of them make it. The daisies and poppies dominated at first as is their wont, but the other species have come through; for brief periods when the flowers bloom it can look convincing, and when we mow it you get that lovely warm hay smell as the grass dries. It looks less like a living, loving monument to a cherished past than a thwarted, well-meaning attempt. I could end the book with me and my dad sowing the seed, lovely and neat; unfortunately real life twists and tricks and rambles on like cornbine or goosegrass, and tends not to end up as tidily as stories do.

BIRDSFOOT TREFOIL

But without trying to draw a Disneyish moral from all this, I think I can paradoxically take a little bit of pleasure from all this. I disabused myself of some naïve ideas about the environment for a start, and I enjoyed my afternoon riding on the tractor with Mal, and mending the mower with my brother. And as the failure gets ever more obvious, as the nettles soar and the docks thicken, I enjoy the adversarial, conspiratorial tones of the conversations I have with people with ruses for getting rid of them. I feel on the same side, us against... *it.* What I've really learned is not stuff about actual growing, but about people; when you're involved with the natural environment around you, you inevitably get involved with the people around you as well; you slip outside that modern process whereby all settlements become more like gated suburban communities, and all workplaces are sealed off and distant. You can learn that embarrassment and failure are not things that you suffer alone, isolated and lonely in a bedroom, but things that unite us all, and form a common bond of humanity between us all. 🐌

Illustrations taken from *The Illustrated Encyclopedia of Wild Flowers* published by Chancellor Press, 1992.

RAGGED ROBIN

It's Easy Being Green

STEPHAN HARDING SAYS THAT DOING NOTHING WILL SAVE THE WORLD. PICS BY ANDREW COUNCIL

Our climate is changing, and if we keep on destroying wild nature and emitting greenhouse gasses into the air there will be dire consequences around the world. In Britain, by mid-century we will suffer from major droughts and heatwaves in summer. Our soils will dry out. Hose pipe bans will be imposed, and there will be less water to dilute dangerous pollutants in our rivers. Imagine winter rains of an intensity

TRIBAL PEOPLE ALL
OVER THE WORLD
WERE ENGAGED IN
APPARENTLY "IDLE"
ACTIVITIES SUCH
AS CEREMONY,
RITUAL AND
MEDITATION

normally seen only in the monsoon-prone tropics. Imagine the flooding, the soil erosion, the land slippage, and the incapacity of our existing sewer networks to deal with the vast volumes of water. Imagine how pest species such as the grey squirrel, the dreaded Phytopthera fungus and new pests never seen before in the UK will severely impact our woodlands and our farmland crops. Imagine some of our favourite beaches and coastal scenery disappearing under the waves as the sea level rises.

The UK is very likely to experience these effects, and many more, as our climate changes. Some changes will appear to be beneficial–there will be more summer sunshine–but most will be detrimental. The changes could come very soon. Indeed, my own experience as a long-term resident of south-west England is that the changes are already happening.

There is now virtually no doubt that the planet as a whole is going through a massive upheaval involving severe disruption not just to climate, but also to our ways of living and to the lives of the millions of species with which we share our planet. Here are two facts that can help us focus our minds on the immensity of what is happening. Firstly, the Earth has not experienced average temperatures as high as today's for about 700,000 years. Secondly, we are wiping out our fellow species with a ruthlessness that beggars the imagination–every day we exterminate some 100 species around the world at a rate about 1000 times faster than the natural background rate of extinction. I say all these things not to spread doom and gloom, but to help us to "get real"–to encourage some sober and realistic thinking about what is likely to happen to our planet so that we can take action to limit climate change.

In my work as a founding member of staff and resident teacher at Dartington's Schumacher College, I have spent many years delving into the causes of this global crisis. The immediate causes are obvious and widely agreed upon—a major one is that our burning of fossil fuels is putting greenhouse gasses into the air. But there is a deeper cause that lies not in our outer actions, but in the very way that we have been taught to see the world ever since our childhoods. This is a worldview so dangerous that it has led us to wage an unwitting war on nature that we cannot possibly win, a worldview that we must quickly modify if we are to have any viable future not just as residents of the UK, but as an entire civilisation.

Our death-dealing worldview is this: that our great turning world is no more than a vast dead machine full of "resources" that have value only when they are converted into money. For us, mountains, forests, and the great wild oceans are all dead things that we are free to exploit as we wish without let or hindrance. We have been taught to disregard qualities —to believe that the sense of elation we feel in the mountains or the calm we experience by a sunlit lake are merely our own idiosyncratic subjective impressions that tell us nothing real about the world. Our culture values only quantities such as weight, height, money in the bank, and so on. And we have been taught to think that good citizenship involves buying more and more stuff so that the global economy can grow. But we remain oblivious to the fact that even the seemingly harmless act of buying a trendy new product can help to wreck the planet because of the pollution and habitat destruction involved in the production of just about every single item in our shops and supermarkets.

This death-dealing worldview, which took hold especially strongly during the scientific revolution of the 16th and 17th centuries, is literally laying our world to waste, and is at odds with a more ancient sensibility that saw the Earth as a living being worthy of reverence and respect. Our tribal ancestors felt that they lived within a great psyche, the psyche of the world itself —the *anima mundi*. According to their teachings, this soul of the world deeply affected them with strange promptings from within its unknown depths and was in turn responsive to their prayers and ways of being in the world. Contrary to popular opinion, tribal people all over the world devoted most of their time not to the supposedly harsh strictures of survival (hunting, making shelter etc) but were mostly engaged in apparently "idle" activities such as ceremony, ritual and meditation in order to cultivate and deepen their connection with the *anima mundi*.

Strangely enough, the idea that the Earth is alive has come back to the modern world in an unlikely arena—within science itself. In 1972 James Lovelock, the great British scientist, proposed that our planet consists of a tightly coupled set of complex feedbacks between life, rocks, air and water that gives rise to the emergent ability of the planet as a whole to regulate its own surface conditions within the narrow limits suitable for life.

Inspired by William Golding, Lovelock chose to his name his theory of a self-regulating Earth after Gaia, the ancient Greek divinity of the Earth. A key insight from Gaia theory for us to ponder is that we humans are not in charge of the planet–that we are not the most important of her species. Instead, in the words of Aldo Leopold, the great American environmentalist of the last century, we are "just plain members of the biotic community"–special in our own unique ways, but no more special in principle than the trees, the great whales or the millions of other species that populate our newly stricken world.

Perhaps it is time to counter our dangerously outdated "mechanistic" worldview with a more fruitful, more soulful idea more in tune with the wisdom of our indigenous ancestors. Try it. What if we live inside a great spherical sentient living creature that has been charting her yearly path around the sun for 4,000 million years, evolving her capacity for keeping her crumpled surface suitable for life as her biodiversity has increased over geological time? Her law is that any being that destabilises her climate will experience feedbacks from the whole "system" that will curtail the activities of that being. So we have a choice. We can carry on with business as usual and live in rightful fear of Gaia. Or we can learn to love her hills, her wild forests and her oceans as we love a cherished grandmother. Perhaps only then, motivated by this love of all earthly things, will we find the inspiration for mending our ways and for massively reducing our impact on the great being that gave us birth.

The most important thing we can do in this regard is to develop the Gaian art of doing nothing. What on Earth do I mean? I am talking here about the urgent need for all of us to uncover our deep indigenous connection with the earthly community of rocks, atmosphere, water and living beings–with the animate Earth that enfolds us–for this will give us the energy and insight to do less to save the planet. What does this "doing nothing" consist of? It's very simple, and involves nothing more than laying on your back in a nice place outdoors. I offer you a "meditation". Just try it. I guarantee that it will give you an unexpected wealth of happiness and connection. From the point of view of our mainstream culture you will be "doing nothing", but in fact you will be engaging in a highly subversive act–the demolition of our suicidal and vastly destructive worldview.

Lay on your back on the ground outside in as peaceful a place as you can find, in the forest perhaps, or by the roaring sea. Relax and take a few deep breaths. Now feel the weight of your body on the Earth as the force of gravity holds you down.

Experience gravity as the love that the Earth feels for the very matter that makes up your body, a love that holds you safe and prevents you from floating off into outer space.

Open your eyes and look out into the vast depths of the universe whilst you sense the great bulk of our mother planet at your back. Feel her clasping you to her huge body as she dangles you upside down over the vast cosmos that stretches out below you.

What does it feel like to be held upside down in this way—to feel the depths of space beyond you and the firm grip, almost glue-like grip of the Earth behind you?

Now sense how the Earth curves away beneath your back in all directions. Feel her great continents, her mountain ranges, her oceans, her domains of ice and snow at the poles and her great cloaks of vegetation stretching out from where you are in the great round immensity of her unbelievably diverse body.

Sense her whirling air and her tumbling clouds spinning around her dappled surface.

Breathe in the living immensity of our animate Earth.

When you are ready, get up, breathe deeply, profoundly aware now of the living quality of our planet home.

Do this again and again, at every available opportunity. Let yourself be "Gaia'ed" by the great round sentience of our living world. Persuade your friends, and even your colleagues at work to try it too. Deeply experience what it feels like to meld with the great wild body of our lustrous planet in this way. See how this subtle mode of "doing nothing" can transform your relationship with the whole of life.

Having begun our journey of reconnection, we are ready to engage in doing less in our everyday lives as our contribution to saving the planet. Research by people such as David Reay at the University of Edinburgh has shown that we can make a massive difference in this regard thanks to simple acts such as: turning down our heating in winter by just 1 degree centigrade; using our cars less; composting organic waste; avoiding flying; driving at or below speed limits; eating locally produced food; reducing, reusing and recycling; and by turning off all standbys and transformers. Also, we can have a jolly good think before we buy anything new. We can ask ourselves whether we really need the thing. Could we buy it second-

THE MOST IMPORTANT THING WE CAN DO IS TO DEVELOP THE GAIAN ART OF DOING NOTHING

MAKE MUSIC AND TELL STORIES TOGETHER, RATHER THAN WORK HARD TO BUY USELESS CONSUMER PRODUCTS

hand, or even do without? We can become involved in strengthening our local communities, and find satisfaction in talking, telling stories and making music together rather than in working so mindlessly hard to buy the mostly useless consumer products promoted by the mass media for filling the gaps in our lonely lives. All of this doesn't seem like much, but if enough of us do less in these ways we will make a huge difference, thereby removing the need for several new power stations in the UK.

Strangely enough, connecting with the Earth, consuming less and developing a sense of community can give us the will and energy to work for change on a societal level. In this domain perhaps the most important thing to do is to agitate for a more "idle" global economy—for an economy at steady state that no longer grows by chewing up more and more of the wild, sacred Earth. Those of us touched by Gaia feel the urge to work towards creating an economy in which the only things that grow are non-material "goods" such as love, spirituality and abundant time for laying on our backs in the open air contemplating the wonders of the universe. So, how to move towards this genuinely fruitful kind of growth? We can begin by working less, consuming less and by spending more time outdoors. But we can also lobby government (via our MPs) strongly and rigorously to set a ceiling on greenhouse gas emissions, a move that, amazingly, is being asked for by the business community so they can get on and make massive profits out of selling the new technologies required to meet the new regulations. What business is demanding, you see, is a level playing field—and only government can give it to them. We can also work to persuade our governments to take climate change seriously by giving significant tax breaks and other incentives for implementing energy saving measures, for massive research efforts into renewable energy and for developing ecologically sound ways of food production, building and transportation.

Whilst we engage in these actions, it is important to keep honing our skills for reconnecting with the animate Earth over and over again. Here is another way of doing this that helps us to delve into the qualities of that invisible substance that gives us life, sound and warmth–the atmosphere.

Lay down on your back outside once again, this time where there is native vegetation, and where you can look up through the canopy of branches and green leaves to the sky beyond.

Now invert your gaze, so that the ground behind you becomes the surface of a lake, and the air playing amongst the branches as you look down becomes water, deliciously translucent and fluid, from which you easily extract life-giving oxygen with every breath.

You are floating on the surface of the lake. Trees have become water plants growing down into the silky water, and it is lovely to look down at them as you float on the surface.

Birds are fish darting through the water plants, or swimming through the deep clear waters beyond; falling leaves are gifts that float up from the depths to where you float on the lake's surface.

When you are ready, "dive" down amongst the leaves and branches that grow into the clear depths of the lake like fronds of kelp. Plunge in amongst their leafy greenness and make contact with the water as it swirls around you.

You are swimming through your mother planet's atmosphere, made for you by myriad living beings, some living in the soil and in the ocean, others on the rocks and in the forests.

Return to the surface, and gaze once again into the crystalline water.

When you are ready, roll over and slowly stand up.

Back in the everyday world, breathe in the nourishing air, and breathe out your own gaseous nourishment in turn to the plants around you.

If you "do nothing" in this way, something extraordinary will happen to you very quickly. A great gift will have been bestowed upon you. Your sense of self will have expanded far beyond your narrow concerns to include everything that exists. You will have encountered the deep realization that there is only one self, which is none other than the great Self of the universe. And you will have realised that only this more intoxicating knowledge can guide us towards a genuinely sustainable relationship with our animate Earth. You will have discovered that doing less really does amount to saving the planet without really trying. ☯

Stephan Harding's Animate Earth: Science Intuition and Gaia, *is published by Green Books*

Things to do today
PAY BILLS
TEACH DOG NEW TRICKS
PHONE EMILIA
WATER CACTUS
LOSE WEIGHT
SIGN UP
YOGA
Important
DRINK NINE GLASSES OF
BE MORE EFFICIENT
WASTE NO TIME
NOTES

Zen and Now

FINDING CONVENTIONAL ZEN TOO MUCH LIKE HARD
WORK, ROB TWIGGER INVENTED ZEN SLACKING.
HERE ARE SOME OF HIS TIPS FOR DOING NOTHING
WELL. ILLUSTRATIONS BY ANKE WECKMANN

1   Less is More

2   More is Less

3   No question the world is mad. You have to be able to drop out of that madness from time to time. Zen slacking is one such way. Conventional Zen is about "just sitting", but in a Japanese way which is, or can be, very uncomfortable. The zen becomes a macho exercise in enduring pain. Before you know it you're starting to go mad again. My Zen slacker teacher (my only bona fide Japanese one) was a Buddhist priest who drank beer for breakfast and taught me how to practise "just sitting" in front of the television. I didn't learn much from him at the time, but over time his example proved enduring. Zen slacking is about doing nothing–but not in a noisy way, in a real way–what better place to do nothing than in front of the TV?

4   My Zen slacking teacher never gave me any koans (tricky zen questions you have to solve to become enlightened.) All he ever said was, "You're already enlightened–now you can forget about it." His other favourite phrase was, "Zen is easy, Zen is easy." I think what he meant was that doing nothing involved not trying too hard. At anything.

5   Don't try harder, try better.

6   There is a way to be in a rush. If you sit in a coffee shop taking your time and doing nothing you can observe the kind of rush other people are in when they pay their bill or buy things from the counter. What kind of rush are you in?

7   What is the sound of one hand clapping is the most famous koan. But if you don't care about the answer then you've already solved it.

8   Trying to go with the flow sometimes works, but often doesn't. To go with the flow you should try to resist it to the maximum. Finally that will make you laugh—when it does you'll find it's easy to go with the flow.

9   When you try to chill out it's more trying than chilling. You'll find that things that are unexpected will still irritate you and then depress you because you realize your cool is skin deep. I'm still working on this one. Going for a long walk is pretty good.

10   Most of us, at various stages in our lives, are ori-entated towards success. We feel that without "suc-cess" we are a failure. It's a feeling that can engulf

you for years, and then you emerge and wonder what all the fuss was about. The Zen slacker way out of feeling burdened by the need to be a success (and the momentary pomposity that comes with momentary success) is to do nothing. Really nothing. As soon as you get the "I'm not a success, maybe I'm a failure" feeling you just keep sitting or standing or leaning and do not move until it goes. You revel in prolonging the doing nothing at all.

11   If people did less there would be less. Of everything.

12   The world is mad. When you engage with the world you often have to go a little mad to get things done. Or so it seems. Another way is simply to wait for the right moment. If you can't, because you're in a rush, then you're not Zen slacking. There is always a right moment. If you wait patiently for it you won't miss it. And even if you do—so what?

13   All food is good.

14   Brainstorming rarely produces good ideas—mostly it just produces a storm of confusion. Or else you get ideas as a kind of insurance against being bereft of ideas. These ideas are actually symbolic ideas. But real ideas are there to become real. They have a reality already integral within them. These ideas just come from nowhere because they are looking for you. If you do nothing the solution will come looking for you.

15   Often the best way to start doing nothing is to do something in a consciously excessive way. Excessively write notes until you are sick of that and then you are doing nothing in the right way. No strain anymore.

16   Make a joke against something you hold most dear.

17   Don't ask why the world is mad—it just is.

18   You think you need more money. What you need is to be more in the present. Wanting more money

is being rooted in a future fixated frame of mind. You are hardly alive in such a state of mind. The feeling of desperately wanting money (not food or water- that's different and real) is a good reminder that you are moving too far ahead in time too quickly. You're literally on another planet. This is the mad world, not the now world. To stop worrying about money isn't always easy. One way is to sit and try and force yourself for an hour to think of as many ways to make money as possible– the more stressful as well as the eminently dull and sensible. Sicken yourself with money lust–then have another cup of tea and a biscuit and look out of the window at the world.

19   Find a good place to do nothing. Find good people to do nothing with. Do nothing as often as is bearable.

20   Something always comes out of nothing.

21   Do things that need willpower everyday or on a day you have designated "shit day". Prepare for that shitty day by reminding yourself about it.

22   What will be written on your tombstone?

23   If you find you are too stressed to take phonecalls from old friends then the next time it happens deliberately prolong the call until they are the one to end it.

24   When you find yourself getting that "trying hard" feeling, take a pause and try less hard. Drop down a gear.

25   Is your calm skin deep?

26   Don't take your time, take the right moment.

27   Rely on coincidence. Take confidence from good coincidences, beginner's luck. If everything is against you have a cup of tea and look out of the window at the mad world outside.

28   Are you happy? If you're not sure then you need to do more Zen slacking. Stay on the bus a few stops too far and then amble back.

29   Sometimes things don't work.

30   If you are slightly depressed observe it and revel in it for as long as you can.

31   Aim to watch a bad movie at least once a week. Preferably one you've seen and dismissed before.

32   Whenever you feel competitive, strive to win, in a way that lacks all subtlety.

33   To get up early, sleep in an uncomfortable bed with not enough blankets but make sure the room is warm.

34   Force yourself to stay up late reading a book until it's finished.

35   Revel in the Bee Gees.

36   Give small tips when you feel a strange and unwelcome vibe from an absent waiter that you should tip big because you are such a nice person.

37   Doing good is acting now. Except when it isn't.

38   Be a prat in front of people you don't care about.

39   When you can do nothing, do nothing. But make yourself comfortable. Have a gin and tonic and talk about something lofty and refined.

40   Enlightenment is a decision.

41   Try fishing with a bow and arrow. Or, at least think about fishing with a bow and arrow. Imagine how clear the water would have to be.

HAVE A GIN AND TONIC AND TALK ABOUT
SOMETHING LOFTY AND REFINED

TELL PEOPLE YOU ARE IN THE MIDDLE OF REINVENTING YOURSELF.

42   Be up on daytime TV.

43   Divorce is just the next stage.

44   Your thoughts are just 1/10 you. The other 9/10 is your physicality and what you do.

45   Observe what you do when nobody is watching. Maybe it's funny.

46   Make something out of nothing.

47   When you feel bad and hopeless get on your knees and prostrate yourself a few times. Find yourself giving thanks in a very general way to nothing in particular.

48   Only exercise in the right clothes.

49   When alone talk vociferously in a foreign accent.

50   Use laziness and doing nothing to combat addiction.

51   Have things handy to throw at the television.

52   Watch the sun break the horizon at dawn at least once a year.

53   Always be out without your mobile if you are supposed to be waiting in for an important phonecall.

54   Enjoy what is offered.

55   Refuse to be impressed by money. Talk about the appeal of yellow clothing instead.

56   If you can do it habitually rather than piously, give away things that come to hand as gifts.

57   Always lie about your age.

58   On forms and CVs include a few pointless lies that are impossible to check.

59   The mad modern world tries to process you. Avoid this by not processing others.

60   Revel in being a recluse. Reflect on the fact that Darwin rarely, if ever, left his house after the age of 35. Tell others you are becoming a recluse.

61   Take an entire day to sew on buttons and mend clothes.

62   Everyone learns how to withhold attention as they get older. They become misers. Give attention to children before they seek it. Give attention to everyone before they seek it.

63   Tell people you are in the middle of reinventing yourself.

64   Wait for something to happen. Don't even make a cup of coffee, just wait. It's good practise.

65   Think from time to time of all the time you wasted by doing something rather than nothing.

66   I spoke to a friend about zenslacking and she said, "Oh, you mean, like being a hippy." But she had missed the point. Zen slacking is an antidote, not a permanent way of life. If everything is going fine and you're enjoying life then you don't need it. Zen slacking is for the bad times, when you get chewed up by life–especially all the nasty falsities of modern life. Zen originated as a corrective exercise. According to many commentators, it wasn't supposed to have become a permanent monastic order. Zen slacking is the same, it isn't there to stop you from doing things or provide a uniform, it's there when you need it, when you need to find space for doing nothing well.

67   Take great pride in doing low status work well.

68 Have one adventure, even a micro adventure, at least once a day. A laugh, my friend calls it—something that combines fun and slight risk in a new way. You can't keep having the same laugh, like bungee jumping. It soon palls.

69 If you can't see the fun in what you do, don't do it.

70 Fun, or laughter, is often the something that comes from nothing.

71 If you find yourself worrying about money put together a worst case scenario picture and forget about it. Tell yourself you'll fight to the last. Drive away the depression with an heroic vision of yourself, then forget about it.

72 When people talk about how much money someone else has, say: "so fucking what?"

73 If having money made people happy surely one of the great religions would have encouraged hoarding, deal making, screwing others over, obsession to the point of damaging yourself and others.

74 Diamond cutters can spend up to six weeks studying a rough diamond to discover the best way to cut. Hit the wrong fault line and it'll smash into a thousand pieces. When you approach something new take the same amount of time and care as a diamond cutter. Keep turning the thing over in your hands. Becomes its friend. Eventually you'll know the right place to apply yourself.

75 How do you "get into" something? Cultivate obsession—but only after you've found what you think is fun about it.

76 You don't need money—you need friends.

77 Zen slacking is for people who have an overdeveloped sense of self-criticism. If you think you're doing fine you don't need Zen slacking.

78 One Saturday get up early, open a beer and read the morning papers. Make sure it's before 9am. Tell people about it.

THINK ABOUT ALL THE TIME YOU WASTED BY DOING SOMETHING RATHER THAN NOTHING

79 People are always saying "Just let go of it". But one way to let go of something is to exaggeratedly hang onto it. This is the point of elaborate mourning rituals in traditional cultures. When you let go you just let go–you can't try to let go. Better to make a great long list of all the benefits of something you want to let go of.

80 It goes without saying that you should take responsibility and not blame others for your situation. But that doesn't mean blaming yourself instead.

81 When you do nothing well you always notice interesting things. Sometimes these can be useful to you. Doing nothing well increases your luck.

82 When you think you haven't got enough time then you are living in the future too much. You're more interested in finishing projects than doing them. If something is better to have done than to do then you probably shouldn't do it.

83 Responsibility doesn't reduce the possibility of having fun, it's wanting to avoid the responsibility that lands on your shoulders that drives fun away.

84 Compliment people on their shoes.

85 Next time you pass a wastebin with something interesting poking out of it retrieve it and make something out of it. A joke or a gift or simply something to examine for a while.

86 Less may not always be more but less leaves you more time. To do nothing well. ◉

Green Men

THE NATURE SPRITE IS ALIVE AND WELL

A figure who combines man and nature is a frequent symbol in most cultures. In England, the Green Man myth is traditionally embodied in Robin Hood, a sort of wild outcast who is tune with the forest and attacks authority. Another sort of Green Man is frequently seen on medieval churches and cathedrals: an impish sprite with tendrils and leaves growing from its mouth and ears. The myth of the avenging spirit of the woods is continually reworked by successive generations, and here we reproduce a few of our favourite green men, from Alan Moore's Swamp Thing to Shrek.

DESIGN FOR A PUB SIGN BY PETE LOVEDAY

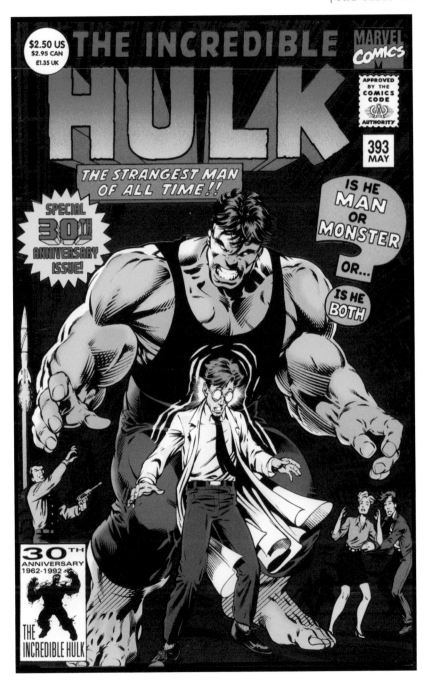

MARVEL COMICS BROUGHT US THE GREEN MAN IN THE SHAPE OF THE HULK

ALAN MOORE'S CREATION SWAMP THING COMBINED AN AVENGING SPIRIT OF NATURE WITH A
SOPHISTICATED INTELLECT

THE JOLLY GREEN GIANT PROMISES A BOUNTIFUL CROP

SHREK AVENGES A GOVERNMENT WHICH TRIES TO OPPRESS NATURE AND THE WILD THINGS

RAYMOND BRIGGS' GLORIOUS ATTACK ON VICTORIAN VALUES

THE GREEN MAN LIVES EVEN AMONGST THE DELUDED STRIVERS OF MAMMON: PUB SIGN IN THE CITY

THIS ROBIN HOOD IMAGE POPS UP IN CLIPART

Junk Food

CAN A BANQUET BE FOUND IN OUR BINS?
FREEGANS THINK SO.
TEXT AND PHOTOGRAPHS BY ALAN CAMPBELL

It's six o'clock on a Tuesday night and as the majority of people I pass are hurrying home to loved ones, scuttling off to the gym or wondering if they should stop off at the pub for a quick one, I'm heading out to find my evening meal. I don't mean I'm going out to dinner in a restaurant, or I'm heading to a fast food place to indulge in the guilty pleasures of a burger and "fries". What I mean is that I'm looking for the food that supermarkets, cafes and restaurants have discarded – items that are past their sell-by dates, fruit that's bruised, packets that are ripped and can't be sold in the store.

But I'm not homeless, and its not that I can't afford to buy these items from the shops, no, far from it. I am, in fact, living as a freegan. Whilst removing food from bins was once seen as something that was solely the preserve of tramps, it is now becoming far more of a lifestyle choice and a political statement.

Freeganism began in North American as an offshoot of the anti-capitalist movement with freegans pulling ample amounts of free food from the bins of supermarkets, restaurants and other food establishments. The word freegan itself is a mixture of "free" and "vegan". These American freegans see this as a way to undermine the profits of firms that treat workers badly, exploit animal rights and contribute to landfill waste sites. One freegan has even gone as far as converting his car to run on discarded oil from restaurants and claims around 12 miles to the gallon.

Despite the name "freegan" being derived in part from vegan, many freegans are meat eaters, although the more cautious are eager to point out that the dangers of eating meat and fish recovered

"WE WON'T BUY YOUR CRAP BUT WE WILL EAT YOUR SCRAP"

from bins are great, many still happily cook found meat. The movement is also closely associated to dumpster diving, where divers remove useful items from dumpsters. For many dumpster divers that has included finds such as computers, typewriters, desks, chairs and whole host of other goodies including electrical equipment and designer clothes.

One phrase, which seems to typify the American freegan movement, and has been adopted by one of the freegan organisations, is: "we won't buy your crap, but we will eat your scrap."

In the UK, the freegan movement is boosted by the fact that 17 million tonnes of food are buried in landfill every year, around 4 million tonnes of which are edible. For many in the food industry, the cheapest option is disposal.

So here I am on a Tuesday night in Edinburgh, rooting through bins, trying to salvage what I can. The first few bins I try prove to be nothing more than office detritus" sandwich wrappers, coffee cups and old newspapers. At the back of pub aimed at tourists, I hit the jackpot–grapefruits, limes and lemons. This would certainly ward off scurvy but it hardly makes a meal.

After the initial shock of approaching bins and ripping open bin bags, the whole experience isn't actually too unpleasant. Sure, many of the bins emit a pungent aroma that I know is going to stay with me for a few hours, but beyond that, it's not as awful as you'd think.

The next bin that has anything worth salvaging has enough for several people to eat well for a couple of days. This bin, at the back of a branch of Caffé Nero, has a great deal of sandwiches ranging from egg mayonnaise to wild salmon. It also has about eight pots of rather nice looking soup, about 200 packets of crisps, chocolate, peanuts and other snacks. The surprise find of this bin are a number of pots of fruit salad, all of which look very tasty and were on the shelves in the shop less than an hour before.

The next day I decide to try the supermarkets figuring that with more stock being thrown away,

THE NATURAL HABITAT OF THE FREEGAN AND
SOME OF THE UNSPOILT SPOILS ON OFFER

For More Information

- www.freegan.info
- www.dumpsterworld.com
- www.scavengeuk.mine.nu

I would increase my chances of more exotic findings. After a few hours spent going from one supermarket to the next, I give up. It seems that the larger supermarkets have pre-empted freegans and located their bins behind locked doors or in locked yards.

Contrary to appearances, the main supermarkets and high street sandwich bars do have a policy on the disposal of edible food. Prêt A Manger works with the charity Crisis Fairshare in London and in the past year has donated nine tonnes of food to them, the equivalent to 264,000 meals. Local Prêt A Manger stores may not have agreements in place with any local charity, but the firm has taken the step of appointing a sustainability manager that is charged with implementing agreements wherever possible. Supermarket giant Sainsbury's has been donating food to charity since 1998. In the period 2003-2004, 245 of their stores, that's about half of the current number of UK stores, donated food worth £3.9 million. Last year, Sainsbury's claim to have donated 7,250 tonnes of food.

THE CONTENTS OF THIS BIN COULD WARD OFF SCURVY BUT HARDLY MAKE A MEAL

Technically, removing food from bins is theft and I am making myself liable to prosecution by openly rummaging around in bins in broad daylight. The lawyers that I spoke to prior to my foray into freeganism found the idea of prosecution of someone taking edible food from a bin somewhat laughable. They were at pains to point out that while I was committing a crime, the result of my actions were far from detrimental to anyone, although they did reiterate that if I got food poisoning from anything I'd eaten, it would be impossible to sue the offending organisation.

Perhaps the oddest part of the whole freegan experience, apart from the initial apprehension I felt at rooting around in the rubbish, was the reaction of people who passed me by. In many places, freegans operate under the cover of dark to preserve anonymity and minimise the amount of potential contact with others. I chose to conduct my hunt when I knew people would be around as I was interested in their reactions to my foraging. Of the few people that passed me, not one said anything or appeared even slightly curious in what I was doing.

My experiment into freeganism lasted about three days, and while that is a short space of time, it did change the way I look at the amount of waste we generate every single day and how much of it could be diverted to other sources. There's no doubt that being a freegan is a great deal more work than buying food and that increased amount of work is enough to put off most people. Ultimately, what I found was food that was exactly the same as you'd buy, the only difference being that it was free. ◉

AROUND FOUR MILLION TONNES OF EDIBLE FOOD ARE BURIED EVERY YEAR IN THE UK

How to be a freegan

- Take gloves and a torch.
- Always leave the bin and surrounding area as clean as you found it.
- Use discretion when choosing what to eat. If in doubt, throw it out.
- If the bag is ripped or any food items are exposed, just leave them behind.
- Just because a bin is no good one day, doesn't mean it will be like that every day.
- In general small to medium shops are probably best. Larger chains have their bins locked away.
- Wash all the items you find before consuming.
- Respect "No Entry" and "No Trespassing" signs.

Tips for Tat

WHEN KITTING OUT YOUR NEW FLAT, AVOID IKEA AND GO FOR THE SKIPS, ADVISES ASH PROSSER. ILLUSTRATION BY HANNAH DYSON.

As the Situationists remind us: "Ne Travaillez Jamais!" However, if you don't work, you tend to have very little money, and if you have very little money then your chances of having the things that you want are minimised. There are two paths to go down with desire. Either put an awful lot of effort into ridding yourself of them by meditating for hours, diving into cold lakes, sitting in caves, humming a lot and not having any sex, or put all that effort into some form of work which will give you the money to realise them. Whichever path you choose, the ratio of work done to desires realised is often too low to make the effort worthwhile.

Better, as ever, to find the some useful middle path. Instead of working for money to realise your desires, put all that effort into offering yourself to the fates. If it's stuff you want, guaranteed it's out there somewhere. You just have to find it. Now, the holiest of men (aka pure idlers) will literally sit and do nothing all day and whatever they need will be brought to them.

For most contemporary idlers, though, the luxury of such minimal need is a long way off.

IN THE TRADITION
OF THE WOMBLES,
WE MAKE GOOD USE
OF THE THINGS
THAT WE FIND,
THINGS THAT THE
EVERYDAY FOLK
LEAVE BEHIND

If you want to live in the city, swan about looking cool and get yourself kitted out with all the vital accoutrements of everyday Babylonian living, then you are going to need to go tatting.

Tatting is the seeking for objects of usefulness in among the tat that is left behind by the mob. Bins, skips, a field after a festival, anywhere where there is evidence of human consumption, there will be waste. One person's waste is another's treasure, and, in among the dross, pearls will surely come forth.

In the true alchemical tradition of the Wombles, tatting consists of "making good use of the things that we find, things that the everyday folk leave behind." Tatting works best in the urban realm, where there are people and consumer durables in abundance. Most of the latter have built-in obsolescence—they are constructed to fade out or break down in a very short space of time. Fashion and fad

are the supports upon which the tatter builds an empire—whenever something becomes outmoded, it is discarded to be replaced with the latest up-to-date model. That which is cast-off becomes the building blocks of the tatter's world- a life lived off the scraps.

The first rule of tatting is that whenever you are out and about, keep your eyes peeled for stuff. The streets might not be paved with gold, but there are plenty of dropped items that will catch the discerning tatter's eye during random wanders through the cityscape. Clothes are often discarded, meaning a misplaced scarf here and a dropped hat there will furnish the tatter's wardrobe for many a winter to come. Going through the town after a Saturday night is a valuable source of abandoned apparel. Drunken revellers and sweating clubbers will cast off t-shirts and shoes with Dionysian relish as their altered state of consciousness takes them into long-forgotten realms of spontaneous nudity. Such victims of the cup of life are to the tatter what the tailors of Savile Row are to the well-heeled businessman—a source of interesting and varied clobber, with one crucial difference: the tatter is dressed for nothing.

Many who tat for clothes will mix and match their finds to create new and exciting fashion statements. Tatters are truly clad in motley, their coats of many colours a visible sign of their dedication to the gypsy way, and the tradition is acknowledged among tatters who will boast of how their entire collection of clothes was either given to them or found along the way. When out on the town dressed top to toe in an entirely found get-up, there is a certain sense of smugness for the tatter, who looks just as good as anyone else, but at no cost.

Beyond the streets themselves are the bins and skips. These are the lifeblood of the tatter, the arks of the covenant of the idle. One of the first rules of the enlightened is that whatever you might want is already there—you just need to find it. Recently, your author moved house. Being a man of, at least to some degree, truth, he had cast off all his possessions in a long, and often quite boring, quest to find ultimate freedom. However, this version of life can become a little slow when you find yourself in a bare flat, staring at the four walls (because you've only *got* the four walls and nothing within them) wondering why no one comes to visit you in your half-baked monastic cell of heavy austerity and misplaced asceticism.

Tired of that, I hit the streets. Bins outside the backs of charity shops are the best. The masses buy, get fed up with and then give to the charity shop. The charity shop collects an absurd amount of stuff that no one wants any more, they can't sell it all, so they bin it. It is upon these bins that a whole swarm of latter-day roma descend, a transformative plague of the drop-outs, the retired and the dispossessed who seek the holy grails of functional domestic respectability for free. So I needed a rug. Off to the bin, pull open a few plastic bags, and presto! A big beautiful red rug now brightens up the cell. Next, a table upon which to write the Great Works. Outside the back of an Oxfam, an old school desk turns up, complete with sunken ink-well and lift-up top. The flat I moved into had no kitchenware save for a couple of cups and a plate. Within a week I have a complete cutlery set, three teapots of varying shapes and sizes, enough crockery items to open a small café, plenty of pots and pans, one of those plastic draining-board things and a top-of-the-range perfect-working-order toaster. All for nothing, all out of the bins.

Eventually, as you tune in with the magic bin, you start getting precisely what you want. My radio cassette player broke, so off to the bins to find a radio cassette player. The weather's a bit chilly, I need an extra duvet or blanket, so it's off to the magic bin to bring home the booty.

When tatting, there are certain rules of engagement to follow. If you arrive at a bin that is already being tatted, wait your turn. No tatter likes someone barging in and diving around in the bin while he is having his own good rummage. Listen out for tips—tatters will swap notes about which bins have been cleaned out, and which might have some decent stuff left in there. Pick your times to tat—early mornings before the bin men arrive and twilight when the shops throw out are the good times. Take a decent-sized bag to carry home your treasure, and never be greedy. Be prepared also to get down and dirty. Most tatters will know that many of the best finds are right at the bottom of the bin. In many cases, it's best to actually jump *into* it to get what you really want.

Of course, one great thing about tatting is that you are no longer feeding The Machine. It's all very well going on marches to protest about capitalism while wearing trainers you bought brand-new from a shop. Such hypocrisy can be alleviated by following the simple rule—never buy anything. If you absolutely cannot manifest or scavenge for what you want, buy from a charity shop—at least that way you are using the stuff that has already been produced and not encouraging yet more consumerism. Tatting is fun and a good way to meet others like yourself—those who continue to practise the everyday miracle that is getting something for nothing. ◉

THE IDLER

UKULELE SPECIAL

Why Uke?

A VERY SPECIAL READER SENT US THIS INTRODUCTION TO THE MAGICAL LITTLE FOUR-STRING FRIEND, INSPIRING THIS WHOLE SECTION

As soon as you tell anyone you play the ukulele, they will either mention Tiny Tim or, worse, George Formby. Mentioning Tiny Tim to me is likely to get you a swift boot in the Cratchetts, whereas mention of George Formby is liable to inspire me to do a passable impression of George Foreman instead (and I'm not talking about knocking you up a mixed grill).

For one thing, Formby favoured the "banjolele", a far more strident and irritating instrument than the sweet little guitar-shaped "figure 8" Secondly, it conjures up images of wartime austerity, music hall and not-very-funny humorous ditties. This does a fine instrument a gross disservice. The ukulele is much maligned and misunderstood.

Indeed, the uke could have been custom made to fit with an idling lifestyle; it is the perfect instrument for idlers (if not the perfect instrument, full stop). Please forgive my evangelical tone, but I feel that it's my duty to explain why.

First off, there's the price. Many people express an interest in learning an instrument, but we're put off by the prohibitive prices of actually buying one. Even second hand, a barely decent guitar, woodwind instrument or keyboard won't leave much change from £200 (and forget about brass or drums), whereas you can buy a perfectly playable uke with £15 in your pocket, and still pay for your lunch and bus fares with the change (in fact,

> THE UKE CAN
> BE CARRIED
> ANYWHERE
> AND PLAYED
> ANYWHERE:
> WHILE SMOKING,
> DRINKING,

I recently bought a uke for my daughter and busked with it while waiting for my bus, and by the time the bus came, the uke was paid for).

There are few other instruments in the same price bracket, and none are as versatile as the uke. You can use them as accompaniment to singing (try singing with a tin whistle jammed in your chops), strum something simple, fingerpick some really complex Scott Joplin tune or thrash your way through Nirvana's greatest hits. I've been known to knock out Bohemian Rhapsody, in full, on just voice and ukulele. If you're sceptical, check out the sterling work of the Ukulele Orchestra of Great Britain.

Also, there's the ease of learning. While you may take a while before you sound like Django Reinhart, even a novice can learn a few chords and be playing songs within an hour or two. Some exponents have been known to take spare ukes to gigs and teach backing parts to audience members there and then. An instrument that can be mastered with dedication, yet doesn't demand any real effort to be enjoyed, must be the ideal for idler sensibilities.

Then there's the size. Portable and light, you can comfortably play one in an armchair (arms get in the way with guitars), in bed, in a hammock, in the toilet, on the beach or up a tree. People keep them in the car for playing in traffic jams or in the office filing cabinet for a 9-5 de-stress; they can be slung into a backpack or even a coat pocket; they can be carried anywhere and played standing up, sitting down, lying flat, while smoking, drinking, camping or commuting. Tough luck cellists!

UKULELE SPECIAL

Their size also makes them surprisingly robust: if you do fall asleep and let it slide to the floor, it's doubtful you'll do any damage–I never have. Even if you did, at £12 a pop to replace, who cares?

What with its diminutive size, its price and its sweet little voice, it is often not taken seriously as a "proper"musical instrument. It should carry a label that proclaims: "CAUTION: NOT A TOY."It is anything but. There are some utterly world-class players of the uke out there, such as Canada's James Hill or Japan's Jake Shimabukuro. Their level of virtuosity is nothing short of astounding.

Of course, there is something inherently comic and cheeky about the ukulele too, perhaps even bordering on the bizarre, which is why it is so frequently seen in the hands of stand-up comedians. This association also gives it a certain kudos as an invaluable part of the arsenal of satirists, politicos and malcontents–it is a guerrilla instrument, a concealed weapon.

I take advantage of these attributes within the framework of my own idling lifestyle, slinging the uke on my back, cycling into the city centre and busking whenever I am suffering from a shortage of readies. When I'm not, I don't. Among the Kylie, the Radiohead, the Nirvana and the Abba, I slip in a good few tunes of my own, and most of the material I write extols the virtues of the idle philosophy. So, it kills several birds with one stone: it gives me a steady income with infinite flexibility; it allows me the opportunity to earn doing what I would be doing anyway; it allows me to address the issues of the wage slave/consumption culture on the very front line–at the shops.

I know that could be interpreted as a bit pompous, but you can't be pompous with a uke in your hand–it's just not possible. The simplicity of this unassuming little instrument cuts through swathes of musical and political pretension. It's hard to come over as competitive, "arteestic" or superior if you're toting a uke. And you can't underestimate how damned cheerful it is. Someone once said: "You have to really want to be sad to play the blues on a ukulele" (though, believe me, it is more than possible). It has a well-deserved reputation for being good-natured, uncomplicated, unpretentious, marginalized, misunderstood, subversive, iconoclastic, independent and individualistic; it has an excellent sense of humour, a laconic, quiet voice and is frequently grossly underestimated.

Remind you of anyone? 🐚

Uke 'em All

THIS IS AN EXTRACT FROM A FORTHCOMING BOOK BY BILL DRUMMOND ABOUT THE 17

And so to the Cumberland. Our digs for the time we are in Newcastle is a house in the Sandyford region of the city. It is a Victorian terraced house. Our landlord, David Fry, is a potter. It was him who took us up to the Cumberland for a drink. The pub was fine, the beer was good, the location fantastic. And it seemed to feature live music of some variety every night of the week.

The Cumberland Arms has two rooms on the ground floor; one for drinking and debating and the other for music making. We were drinking and debating. We could hear strains of music from next door. After my second pint of Rapper (the guest ale) I went next door to investigate. The room was no bigger than a moderate front room, a bench around two and a half walls and a scatter of tables and stools. The place was comfortably full of drinkers. From a dapper man in his late 70s to a lass in her early twenties with every age, sexual persuasion and physical type in between. What they all had in common was what they held lovingly to their chests. Each was holding a small but perfectly formed ukulele.

The ukulele is an instrument that had never troubled my imagination even though "Leaning On The Lamppost" by George Formby was the first song I ever heard on the radio. I was aware of that thing called the Ukulele Orchestra Of Great Britain but never heard them. As far as I was concerned the ukulele was a joke. An old one at that.

This lot were singing and playing "Harvest Moon" as written and originally performed by Neil Young. When it ended no one clapped other than me and my comrades. There was no audience other than us. They then chatted

NOTICE

ALL KNOWN MUSIC HAS RUN ITS COURSE.

IT HAS ALL BEEN CONSUMED, TRADED, DOWNLOADED, UNDERSTOOD, HEARD BEFORE, SAMPLED, LEARNED, REVIVED, JUDGED AND FOUND WANTING.

DISPENSE WITH ALL PREVIOUS FORMS OF MUSIC AND MUSIC-MAKING AND START AGAIN.

YEAR ZERO NOW.

The17 IS A CHOIR.

THEIR MUSIC HAS NO HISTORY, FOLLOWS NO TRADITIONS, RECOGNISES NO CONTEMPORARIES.

THE CHOIR HAS MANY VOICES.

THEY USE NO LIBRETTO, LYRICS OR WORDS; NO TIME SIGNATURES, RHYTHM OR BEATS; AND HAVE NO KNOWLEDGE OF MELODY, COUNTERPOINT OR HARMONY.

The17 STRUGGLE WITH THE DARK AND RESPOND TO THE LIGHT.

pb Printout 13   2003

and supped their pints, cups of tea and glasses of orange and then with not even a nod to each other they broke into "King Of The Road". This too came to an end and more chat about this and that, and then another one of them, a large man with a walrus moustache, broke into a version of "Flowers In The Rain".

If, like me, you were lying in bed on the 30th September 1967, with your radio tuned to 247 on the medium wave band you would know that "Flowers In The Rain", as written by Roy Wood and performed by The Move was the first record broadcast on Radio 1. On that particular Saturday morning the idea of the reality of Radio 1 seemed so incredibly exciting.

Hearing this ukulele driven version of the same song 38 years and 205 days later had an equally powerful emotional impact on me, back then when it was Tony Blackburn spinning it for the first time as a Radio 1 disc jockey it was upbeat, sunny, full of promise. London was still swinging and now we had Radio 1 the rest of the country was too. This version played by this lot and sung by the large man with the walrus moustache was full of pathos and loss reminding one of a golden era long gone.

We found stools, supped our pints and spent the next hour or so listening to what we learnt were the Ukulele Allstars.

Walking back up the Ouseburn valley to our digs I was forced to admit that I was smitten with this ukulele thing. I wanted to posses one of my very own. I wanted to be in a ukulele orchestra. I wanted to fit in and sing songs and strum along and sup my pint. I wanted to go along every week to rehearsals, week in and week out for the rest of my life. By the time we got back to the digs, it was all settled in my mind. I could have a parallel life to the one where all this "All known music is rubbish…" and The 17 stuff exists. In this parallel life I could have a ukulele, be a regular down at the local ukulele orchestra practise nights, where they would know me only as Tenzing Scott Brown. This Tenzing thing is a *nom de plume* that I have used in the past and have been looking for an excuse to use again. Maybe it would be good for me, like porn is supposed to keep a man's wayward and wandering desires sated thus help him keep faithful to the woman he loves. The ukulele would be my porn, enabling me to stay faithful to the higher aims of what The 17 was all about. Nobody would ever need know, the ukulele could stay hidden under my bed and once a week I could snick out and down to the pub where we practice and all my fellow strummers would only ever know me as Tenzing. And if anybody ever asked how I got such a strange name, I would tell them that I was named after the family cat who every night would climb up the ivy and into the bedroom window, who in turn was named after the Sherpa who conquered Everest. ◉

Uke For Freedom

MATHEW CLAYTON REVEALS THE HISTORY OF THE UKE AS HAWAII'S FAVOURITE INSTRUMENT FOR THOSE WHO PREFERRED NOT TO WORK

In the late 19th century there was a wave of immigration from Portugal to Hawaii. The journey from Europe was long and dangerous so it is not surprising that when a ship called the Ravenscrag docked at Honolulu on the 23rd August 1879, one of its 419 passengers, Joao Fernandes, leapt on to the pier clutching a friend's braguinha (a small guitar popular in Portugal) and began celebrating their arrival by playing some traditional folk songs.

Later that week the *Hawaiian Gazette* noted that the passengers on the Ravenscrag had been delighting people with, "very sweet music" played, "on strange instruments which are a kind of cross between a guitar and banjo."

This was the first time the Hawaiians had heard the braguinha but within ten years it was the most popular instrument on the island, feted by royalty and peasants alike. They modified the instrument slightly and renamed it the ukulele, which means "jumping flea" in Hawaiian. Much of this popularity was down to Fernandes who instead of knuckling down to work in the sugar cane fields spent most of his time wandering round the countryside playing his ukulele, to the great displeasure of his wife.

UKULELE SPECIAL

Also on board the Raavenscrag were three cabinet makers, José do Espirito Santo, Manuel Nunes, and Augusto Dias, who also helped popularise the uke. Like many other cabinet makers of their time they also made musical instruments and by the mid 1880s they had all set up workshops dedicated to making and selling ukuleles.

The next great step in the ukulele history was made in 1915 when the Hawaiian government set up a pavilion at the Panama Pacific International Exposition in San Francisco. Its pavilion featured grass-skirted Hula girls dancing and playing the ukulele. They caused a sensation and soon a fully-fledged Hawaiian music craze had started. In the U.S. players like Ukulele Ike became huge stars and in England George Formby's innuendo laden ditties made him the number one box office draw at the cinema all the way up to the Second World War.

What set the ukulele apart from other popular music trends was that it was about playing and not just listening. It was also particularly suited to the music of that age. If you play a chord on the ukulele it lacks sustain (like you would find on a guitar) giving everything a naturally jaunty, bouncy rhythmic feel that was inherent in music of the 20s and 30s.

It is also fitting that the first burst of ukulele playing by Fernandes on the dock all those years ago was intended as a cheerful celebration as it is this spirit that the instrument still manages to convey so well today over 100 years later. ◉

THE UKULELE IS ABOUT PLAYING, NOT JUST LISTENING

Buying a uke

BEFORE YOU RUSH OUT TO INDULGE YOUR NEW HOBBY, READ MATHEW CLAYTON'S BUYER'S GUIDE

1 You don't need to spend a fortune on a uke but you will find it more enjoyable if you don't buy the cheapest as these go out of tune continually. Around £30-40 will get you a decent one. There are many reputable brands; the best place to buy one from is your local music shop rather than a toy store.

2 There are a number of types of uke all different sizes, which can be confusing, but the standard is the "soprano".

3 The "concert" and the "tenor" sounds pretty much the same but are a little bigger so you might consider these if you find it difficult to fit all your fingers on the fret board of the soprano.

4 The "baritone" is larger still, it is normally strung just like the top four strings of a guitar (DGBE) so is great for guitar players as you don't need to learn any new chords. The downside is that it doesn't have the distinctive uke sound as the top string has the lowest rather then the highest pitch. Tuning the top string higher than the others is called "re-entrant" and is what makes the uke sound a little like a banjo.

5 Two less common types of uke are the banjulele which has more of a twang to it

DUKE OF UKE OWNER MATTHEW REYNOLDS TAKES A BREAK FROM PUSHING BROOM

and looks like a little banjo and the resonator uke which looks like a small-scale steel guitar.

6 You might also come across Flukes and Fleas; these are actually a make of ukulele rather than a type but look a little different as they are based on a pineapple rather than figure of eight shape. The have a part plastic rather than all wood body but don't let this put you off. They still sound great.

7 Most models also come in semi-acoustic versions so you can plug them into an amplifier but these cost a little more.

8 Ask the shop assistant to tune the uke before you try playing it.

9 Buying an electronic tuner will save you considerable frustration later on. You don't need an expensive model, the cheaper ones cost about a tenner. Ask the man in the music shop to show you how it works before you buy it. It may seem like an unnecessary expense but it is really worth it.

10 You can get hard or soft cases for ukuleles, soft cases are cheaper but great as they normally come with straps and you can wear the ukulele on your back like a rucksack and carry it anywhere. 🎱

How to Play

HERE ARE THE CHORDS.
NOW START A UKULELE
ORCHESTRA

Master a few chords and you can be playing the great hits in next to no time. Chord patterns are easily available from music shops, on the Internet, or just by listening to the song and working it out. Teenage Kicks by The Undertones, for example, uses just C, Am, F and G.

First Lesson
CHORDS REQUIRED C, F

1 Count evenly from 1 to 8

2 Play a down stroke across all the strings whilst holding a C chord as you say each number

3 Now play an F chord as you say each number. Practice until you can move between the two chords easily. So you are playing C from 1 to 8 then F from 1 to 8 and back to C again etc.

4 In between counting each number say "and". So 1 and 2 and 3 and 4 and etc. The "and" is known as the offbeat (you will recognise the off-beat from dance music, it is where you hear the "tssk" of the hi hat whilst the bass drum falls on the number or the on beat e.g. boom tssk boom tssk etc).

5 Now try adding an upstroke. Start by playing it on the "and" in between beats 7 and 8.

6 Once you are comfortable with this add another upstroke one the offbeat "and" between beats 3 and 4.

7 From here the world is your oyster. Start experimenting by adding more upstrokes on the offbeat or changing down strokes into upstrokes. NB repeat exactly the same pattern of up/down on/offbeat strums on the C and then the F as this will give it a groove.

UKULELE SPECIAL

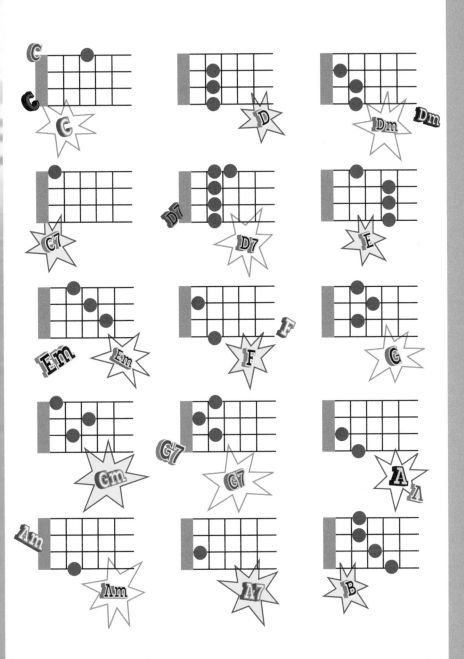

UKULELE SPECIAL

Second Lesson
CHORDS REQUIRED C, F

1 This time we will be playing the same chords C and F and will again be counting but instead of strumming you are going to pick

2 Start by holding a C chord and plucking the bottom or 4th string (the one nearest your shoes) as you say one, then the top or 1st string as you say two, then the 3rd string as you say three, then the 1st string as you say four

3 Repeat this pattern

4 Now try the same pattern whilst holding an F shape

5 Repeat this pattern

6 Now try playing it continually whilst alternating smoothly between chords

UKULELE SPECIAL

Third Lesson
Chords required: C, D7, Cmaj

1 For this lesson we are going to try a barre chord. This is when you put your index finger across all the strings and hold them all down.

2 We will start by playing a C chord, make sure you use your middle finger to hold down the note.

3 Play a down stroke on the on beat as you count to 1 to 8

4 For your next cycle of 8 beats put your index finger across all the strings a fret below (nearer the tuning pegs). Keep your middle finger holding down the bottom string. Again play a down stroke on each on beat.
   This is a D7 chord

5 Repeat this cycle of 2 chords 3 times and then finish with 8 on beats of a C maj chord (see diagram)

6 Start counting "and" in the offbeat and add your own up and down stroke variations

Fourth Lesson
Chords required: C, C7, F, G7

1 The ukulele sounds great when playing "7" chords. For this lesson we are going to try two new "7" chords.

2 Once you are familiar with the chord shapes starting playing them, one down stroke per beat in the following pattern.

3 C for 8 beats, C7 for 8 beats, F for 4 beats, G7 for beats back to again C again.

4 Start adding your own offbeat and upstroke variations. ◉

You can play the uke!

Uke Resources

By Mathew Clayton

Events

Ukulele Orchestra of Great Britain Workshops

These happen every couple of months and are organised ny the brilliant UOGB at Cecil Sharp House in London and are aimed at individuals who want to try playing in a large group. Details at www.ukuleleorchestra.com/main/home.aspx

Uke Joint

Run by the lovely Robert Austin this is a bi-monthly ukulele night in a room above a pub on the Euston Road, anyone is free to turn up and play. Details at www.ukejoint.co.uk

Duke of Uke

Fantastic shop on Brick Lane regularly holds events at their shop and around Shoreditch. Details at www.dukeofuke.co.uk

Books

Jumpin' Jim's Ukulele Beach Party
Jumpin' Jim's '60s Uke-In

Jumpin Jim is Jim Beloff who has compiled a whole series of uke songbooks, the two above contain a variety of surf and Beatles classics. You can find all on amazon. He is also the man behind the wonderful Fluke and Flea ukuleles. His website is www.fleamarketmusic.com

Players

Dulwich Ukulele Club

Aka the Duc—this is the band I am in. There are eight uke players and the extraordinarily talented duo of Zed on percussion and Pete on Xylophone. We are available for Blues, Beanos and Bar mitzvahs contact: www.theduc.org/

UKULELE SPECIAL

NIPPER
aka Tim Lewis is a Somerset based music teacher who has over 70 ukulele students. He also plays ukulele infused reggae, which you can download from www.ukeland.com/~nipper/ep/

YOUTUBE.COM
Features a whole bunch of great ukulele player and short films from home made animation to vintage performances, highlights include the Ukulele Orchestra of Great Britain performing "Smells like Teen Spirit". Just type ukulele into the search engine.

Blogs

UKELELIA
Your passport to 4-string paradise, co written by Mark Frauenfelder founder of cool cyber journal Boing Boing. www.ukulelia.com

UKE CLUB
Written by cartoonist D.J. Coffman, this lively blog combines his love of ukes with his love of cartoons. www.yirmumah.net/ukulele

Songs

FLEABAG MUSIC
A collection of public domain songs that have been gathered together so that large uke gatherings will have a shared songbook www.ukulele.org/fleabag.html

ALLIGATOR BOOGALOO
For a slightly more contemporary set of songs that features everyone from the White Stripes to Radiohead go to: www.alligatorboogaloo.com/uke/index.html

Instruction

UKE SCHOOL
Pretty comprehensive lessons that will soon have you playing like Hendrix. www.ukeschool.com/school/levels.html

Community

UK UKE
Ray Shakeshaft's enthusiastic British site amongst other things hosts a bunch of UK players MP3's www.ukuke.co.uk

4TH PEG
American uke community website that also confusingly hosts the forum for the UK uke. www.4thpeg.com

UKE SANITY
Left wing anti Bush ukulele protest group www.ukesanity.org/about.htm

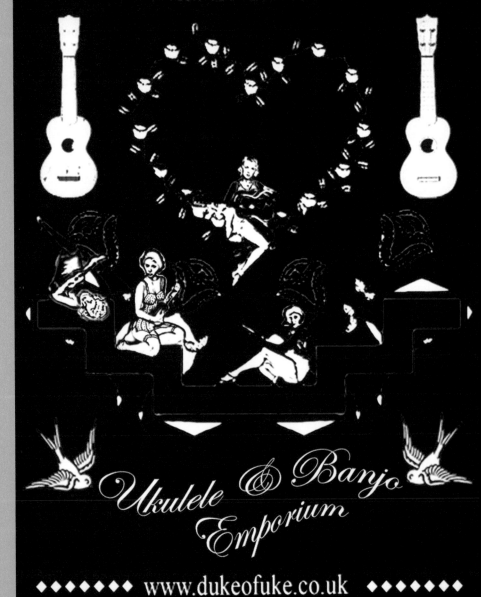

UKULELE SPECIAL

WIN A UKE AND ACCESSORIES WORTH £200!

We have a special limited edition Duke of Uke branded ukelele to be won by a lucky reader. Made in Portugal by top luthier Antonio Pinto specially for the Duke of Uke, the uke has a solid koa and top, back and sides, and we're throwing in a limited edition gig bag made in London by Tatty Devine for the Duke of Uke. The package is worth £200.

JUST ANSWER THE FOLLOWING QUESTION:
WHAT DOES UKULELE LITERALLY MEAN IN HAWAIIAN?

Send your answers to:
tom@idler.co.uk, subject line"uke comp"
or The Idler Uke Comp, The Idler, Studio 20,
24-28a Hatton Wall, London EC1N 8JH.
Closing date: January 31, 2007.

Tatty Devine, 236 Brick Lane,
London, E2 7EB. tel. 020 7739 9009
www.myspace.com/tatty_devine

STORIES

THE TIPPING POINT

THE SATURDAY OF ENGLAND'S WORLD CUP DEFEAT;
THE HOTTEST DAY OF THE YEAR; AN URBAN
SWIMMING HOLE FAR FROM OXFORD'S TOURIST SPIRES.
SO HOT THE CONCRETE'S CRACKING. IAN McEWAN
WEATHER (FINN), LIKE SOMETHING'S GOING TO
HAPPEN... THE WEEDS ARE BURSTING THROUGH
THE PAVEMENT. THE WATER'S COLD AND THICK.
SUSPENDED, WITH ONLY YOUR EYES ABOVE WATER
THE HORIZON SEEMS CIRCULAR.
NOTHING ELSE EXISTS.

BEAUTIFUL DUTCH
TEENAGERS WHO, WIERDLY,
BEGIN PLAYING BADMINTON

BECKHAM 7

"THESE ARE
TOO SMALL—
WE THROW
THEM BACK"

POET KATE

IN HER 'COME
TO SUNNY
PRESTATYN'
SWIMSUIT

PRINCESS
VIOLA, 4

MICHAEL, 6.
(CAN DIVE)

FAGS 'N' BAGS

FLO, 6, CAN
NEARLY
SWIM WITH
ARMBANDS.

TOURIST OXFORD – A MILLION MILES AWAY.

LEO, 7

ALBANIAN BOYS FISHING

"EAH, AT HOME WE USED TO GO OUT T NIGHT AND DYNAMITE THE RIVER HUNDREDS OF FISH ALL LEAPING OUT... TODAY WE GOT ABOUT 30."

FINN DOES THE DRUNK WALK INTO THE RIVER TO AMUSE THE CHILDREN. KATE GET'S LEO TO SHOOT HER DEAD AND SHE SLOWLY TOPPLES IN.

YOU CAN SEE THE BLACKBERRIES BEGINNING IN THE MIDDLE OF HE BRAMBLE FLOWERS. SOMETHING IN THE YEAR HAS CHANGED. WE'RE AT THE TIPPING-POINT

BY BADAUDE

THE PRACTICAL IDLER

THE PRACTICAL IDLER

This issue, our practical section looks at the pleasures living in a yurt, drinking green tea and reading William Cobbett. Living the idle life is all about rejecting the empty promises of money and thinking not about what you want but about what you can do without. The less costly and the simpler your life, the less need to work and the more time for loafing, laughing and playing the uke. Riches may look alluring but they bring an awful lot of of hassle with them.

YOUR GUIDE TO THE EASY LIFE

THE PENCIL

The humble pencil is the most beautiful, practical and eco-friendly writing instrument of all, says Tom Hodgkinson

In these days of wasteful multiple plastic biro packs and pens which incorporate flashing lights and which get trodden on and smashed and end up in the garbage, someone really needs to speak up for the humble pencil.

First, there's the undeniable practical nature of the pencil. We all know the story of the difference between NASA and the Russian cosmonauts when it came to making notes in zero gravity. The Americans spent millions of dollars developing a pen which would write upside down. But the Russians? They took a pencil.

Then there is the low cost in its favour. Pencils are virtually free. Other positives: they don't leak and they create no waste. The pencil sharpenings can go on the compost heap and the pencil itself either simply vanishes or can be thrown on the fire.

Pencil marks can be easily erased and therefore you don't need to throw away bits of paper when you make a mistake. I also love the way pencils write: they flow like a river rather than scratching awkwardly like the dreaded biro.

Pencils, too, are infintely varied: from the super hard 2H to the squashy 2B, with good old reliable HB in the middle. I remember at school how familiar I was with the hardness indication system. Which pencil to choose? 2B or not 2B? And what about all those coloured ones? Do you remember those giant Caran D'Ache boxes that the rich kids had?

The pencil is self-reliant; it needs no ink. One potential drawback is the constant need for a pencil sharpener. Around our house there sit many plastic boxes filled with blunt and broken pencils that no one has bothered to sharpen. Still, this is our fault rather than the fault of the technology, and I've found also that a sharp knife will do the job just as well as a pencil sharpener, while also providing a sort of creative pleasure: it is satisfying to whittle away at a pencil. ◑

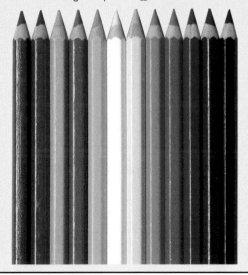

GARDENING

TAKING THE PISS AND TALKING SHIT

The garden: nature's toilet, says Graham Burnett

I t's been said that the next major global conflict is as likely to be fought over water as oil. From this perspective, our habit of using water of drinking quality to flush our bodily wastes out to sea can recognised as the absurdly wasteful practice that it is. Maybe instead we should think about using a "problem is the solution" approach, and find some ways to both preserve our H2O supplies for more vital functions, whilst at the same time actually turning our urine and faeces into valuable sources of fertility.

Peeing straight into the garden is a minimum effort way of providing nitrogen and other nutrients to my growing plants —I often work late at night in the back room, and it's much easier just to pop outside rather than having all the bother of going upstairs and trying not to make a noise that will disturb the rest of the household. Better still if we've got a few friends round for the evening, as long as everyone doesn't go in the same spot. One drawback of urine is that it can actually damage plants if applications are too concentrated —there was also a case I read of in the paper last summer where an otherwise respectable citizen of Middle England was jailed for killing his neighbour's leylandii conifer hedge by systematically pissing on its roots every night. The Centre for Alternative Technology recommends that urine should ideally be watered down by at least 1 part to 10, with their researchers observing that application of this

EDWIN MARNEY

solution led to large increases in brassica and onion crop yields. However, I'm sure that simply moving around and peeing straight onto the soil in different places each time can't do anything but good, and much of the dilution process can be carried out biologically, "in situ" as it were, simply by drinking a few pints of beer during the evening's course. Or else just piss straight onto your compost pile to kick-start the various microbes and bacteria into doing their wonderful job of producing rich organic matter.

Another practical issue is discretion, especially during the daytime, and particularly if you have overlooking neighbours who already consider you "eccentric" to the point of certifiability. Whilst wasting valuable "liquid gold" might seem a shame, a visit to the magistrates court on charges of indecent exposure would be even more regrettable for most of us. I'm lucky in that despite having the small garden of a typical urban terraced house, it's a forest of fruit trees and bushes that can provide me with plenty of cover, or else I can always pop in the greenhouse with a bucket and pretend to be potting something up. I later learned that urine is actually far better used fresh than stored for any length of time anyway, as the nitrogen content quickly turns to ammonia that can actually do more harm than good according to some books, even when used via the compost heap.

A couple of years ago I a received an email from a young chap who had decided to take the logical next step of shitting straight onto his garden, and wanted to know whether this was a practice I'd recommend. I immediately hit "reply" with an emphatic "No! Cease and Desist!! Now!!!" Apart from the questionable aesthetics, fresh human faeces are very likely to carry pathogens that can be extremely harmful to health.

A much better solution would be to build a compost toilet. Here wastes can gently break down over a year or so into pleasantly earthy-smelling "humanure" that can then be applied around fruit bushes and ornamentals rather than salad plants or other leafy vegetables you are likely to directly handle. Unfortunately we don't have room in our garden for such a structure, although I have helped to build one at Dial House, the Essex home of "Camp Idle" as well as our regular permaculture courses. In this particular system the user dumps into a container, covering their deposits with a layer of straw, sawdust or other carbon rich materials. This balances out the high nitrogen content of the faeces, as well as absorbing smells and excess moisture. This mixture is periodically emptied into large wooden compost bins at the end of the garden where its left to get on with its thing until ready. Despite initial misgivings, everybody finds using the toilet most enjoyable. I think this is because we made a conscious effort to avoid the archetypal monuments to squalor often associated with outdoor "facilities". Instead we asked ourselves whether our loo was one that people would feel comfortable about—will it look good, will it smell, and would we feel embarrassed at the thought of visitors using it? Consequently it's not a draughty, stinky nightmare, rather a solid structure where one is happy to take one's time, relax and even sit down and read a good book. Come and try it some time... ◉

THE ANGLER

RUBBISH MEN

Kevin Parr is mystified by the litterbug habits of some of his fellow anglers

I made my first barbel fishing trip of the season yesterday, on a lovely late June afternoon. I watched a red kite's languid flight, saw terns and kingfishers scattering the minnows, and even found time to catch a lovely summer barbel of six and a half pounds.

I should have been floating home after such lovely hours, but my little shoulder bag was weighing me down somewhat—with other people's rubbish.

I can't pretend that I keep the streets clean. Like most people I step over litter on the pavement, looking at the sky while reassuring myself that I'll use my pockets before I dirty the floor. There is also an argument that the grey concrete jungle is brightened by the odd crisp packet, much as the desperate view from an inner city train is enhanced by graffiti art on the stanchions and signal boxes.

A river bank, however, is a very different matter. That water has coursed is path for tens of thousands of years, and nature has adapted itself to its whim. Why anyone, leave alone a fellow angler, can treat such a place with such disregard as to leave two beer cans, a coke can and a Mars wrapper for me to pick-up is as bewildering as it I disgusting. And I do feel genuinely disgusted, especially with the season barely a week old.

As a kid I watched bemused as a local fishing name carefully filled his sandwich bags with stones before chucking them into the pond to sink out of sight. Worse was a guy whose umbrella was being torn apart by a hurricane as I passed him on the way to a weirpool. After a deluge I returned downstream to find he'd abandoned his day—but not his broken brolly, which he'd buried so deeply into brambles beneath a conifer, that I couldn't even reach it, leave alone chase him home with it and burying it up his arse. But for every angler who chucks his bait bags in the hedge there are ninety-nine who will clear up after him. Indeed, the anglers role in the environment is absolutely vital to it. We are the eye and ears of the bankside, natures own policemen.

Just this week I read a story in the local press of a fishermen who spotted fish in distress in his local reservoir in Southampton. He phoned the Environment Agency who arrived to find oxygen levels in the water had fallen to seven per cent in the current drought, oxygen pumps were quickly installed and the fish saved. Had it not been for that phone call, three hundred years of ecology would have disappeared in an instant.

Nobody understands an aquatic environment quite like a fisherman, because no other water user studies it in the same way.

The River Kennet is a prime example. When I first fished

the river, more than fifteen years ago, I was staggered by its vibrancy. It was so alive. Crystal clear, thick with frongs of water-crowfoot, sand-martins feasting on fly hatches at dusk, and the fish! Peering over a high bank was like looking into an aquarium. Loaches and bullhead flitting across the gravel in the shallows, barbel and chub ghosting between the weed in the main flow. But a decade later and everything had changed. Two successive winters of big floods hadn't helped, but excessive water extraction and increased boat traffic were taking their toll. Oxygen levels plummeted, weedgrowth simply vanished, taking with it the larder of insect life and the sanctuary for all things predated. The water changed too. From a glistening sparkle to a green tinged goo. And it was only the fishermen who really noticed. Only they who made any noise. And though the fundamental problems are still there, efforts have been made to cure The Lady of the South. Weed is being replanted and flows monitored.

Anglers point to rapid recaptures and the lack of nerve endings in a fish's mouth as proof that angling isn't cruel, but even they should admit that it would be distressing to be removed by force, albeit temporarily, from their natural habitat.

Please consider our virtues. Rivers like the Don, Dee and Thames, would be little more than open sewers without the money and care generated by anglers. Funding from angling clubs and individuals have secured the safety and development of watery habitat across the country—for everyone to enjoy. And for my part? Well, I once lightened the mood of a Thames Valley copper's nightshift. My evening's fishing was becoming increasingly distracted by the behaviour of the cows in the opposite meadow. They seemed obsessed with eating the thistles sprouting from the river bank some six feet above the river, but the barbed wire fence was creating quite an obstacle. After an hour or so one of the bovines popped its hoof on top of the fence squashing it down and giving better access to the thistles. Half a dozen heifers followed suit, but one had a better idea. Climbing over the fence at a cattle drink upstream the animal inched its way along the precipice until it got its face into the thick of the harvest, to the jealousy of the rest of the herd.

It had to happen, and for the briefest of moments after the bank gave way, the cow stood in fresh air with a quizzical look on its face, before plummeting six feet and creating the biggest splash in history.

The cow swam off downstream, and I followed, slightly anxious that it may find the weir on the bend below me. Instead it found a gravel bar and stood bothered and bedraggled with the remainder of the herd gathered above—a curious audience.

With darkness falling and memories of the impact of Foot and Mouth fresh in my mind, I realised that the farmer might appreciate knowing that one of his prize heifers was waggling its udders in the Kennet.

I called the local police station, promising that this wasn't a wind-up, and retired to bed.

At about one thirty the phone went.

"Mr Parr," the voice came," PC Graham here, Thames Valley Police. I've found the river, now where's this bleedin' cow of yours?" 🐟

TEA TIME

HERBIDACIOUS

Green tea is a favourite for Chris Yates

Especially in summer, I drink almost as much green as ordinary black tea. Refreshing, restorative, re-energising and full of other more mysterious positives, it is possibly as addictive as opium, and much better for me.

Until quite recently, what is now commonly called green tea was only imported into Europe by a few specialist tea freaks, but now you can find stacks of it at your nearest supermarket; and, yesterday, I saw a packet of Clipper Organic Green at my local post office. Of course, the Chinese have been fond of green tea for a while, and the reason they were always ahead of the game has now become obvious: it was three thousand years ago that they first discovered green tea's civilising properties, while here in Europe we were still clubbing each other to death because there wasn't even any PG Tips.

Green tea is green because the leaves are picked when they're young and tender. This makes for a different chemistry to black tea; less tannin, so less of an instant stimulant; more anti-oxidants, more slow-release glow. And green travels better than black. If I take a flask with me when I go fishing or walking, I always fill it with green. Unlike black, it doesn't seem to stew so readily, even when its kept sealed for hours; and so it always tastes fresh, although if you added milk you would destroy both its effect and its personality. Milk is perfectly acceptable with black tea, but pure green tea, made with hot, but not boiling water, needs only itself. Some people drink it chilled, with mint, lemon and ice—but then some people also listen to Barry Manilow.

The Chinese may have been the first to discover it, but in Argentina the Gauchos have been drinking their own particular form of green tea long before they danced the Tango. Mate (pronounced "matay") is a blend of both leaves and stem of a South American herb. It's stonger, more distinctive than China tea, with a slightly smoky, but still superbly refreshing flavour; and it also has many of the spirit-raising qualities of the original, oriental version. Interestingly, my 15-year old son, Will, doesn't appreciate China green, but loves Argentina green. I even had to give him a packet of it so he could he could go off for the weekend and introduce his friends to a new and perfectly legal pleasure. And I nearly always round off my evenings with a cup of the latin.

However, there are are numerous varieties of native green tea, all of them originating in the age of the apothecary. Mint tea (good for indigestion), camomile (good for insomnia), nettle (good for the skin), dandelion leaf (good for the liver), comfrey (good for the nervous system), coriander (the seeds are narcotic), parsley (good for the kidney), angelica (good for coughs). Despite the fact that I've never been fussy about sampling such beverages, some of them can taste like fresh compost. Yet though, for

WILLIAM YATES

taste and refreshment, I definitely prefer the pre-
mier shades of green, there is one more obscure
variety that I always reserve for special occasions,
like when I'm setting out to cast for a particularly
large fish, or when I'm about to begin an important
journey or meet a heart-melting woman. Maybe it's
just my unusual chemistry, but whenever I drink
this unique tea it's as if I had taken a magic potion.
Suddenly I become possessed of a strange yet
unshakeable confidence, and I'm sure that if I had a
notion to fly out of an upstairs window I would glide
serenely for several miles. The tea is very mild, is
not narcotic and grows in ordinary English hedgerows. One day I might harvest and market it and
make a fortune, but until then I shall keep it as my
greenest secret.

TOGETHER IN ELECTRIC DREAMS

THE PASSENGER

WE ARE ELECTRIC

Fanny Johnstone **takes a ride in the Maranello**

In October 2004 a group of graduates and undergrads from Ohio State University designed an electric-powered car called the Buckeye Bullet that reached nearly 315 mph on the Bonneville Salt Flats in Utah and thus breaking the speed record for a completely electric-powered car. But for the moment my first taste of an electric car (apart from the milk float ride with Father Christmas sometime back in the 70s) is the Maranello 4 which goes at 40mph tops and can go fifty miles on one charge. At the time of writing it has only been released in the UK for a month but it's already a prominent presence on London streets.

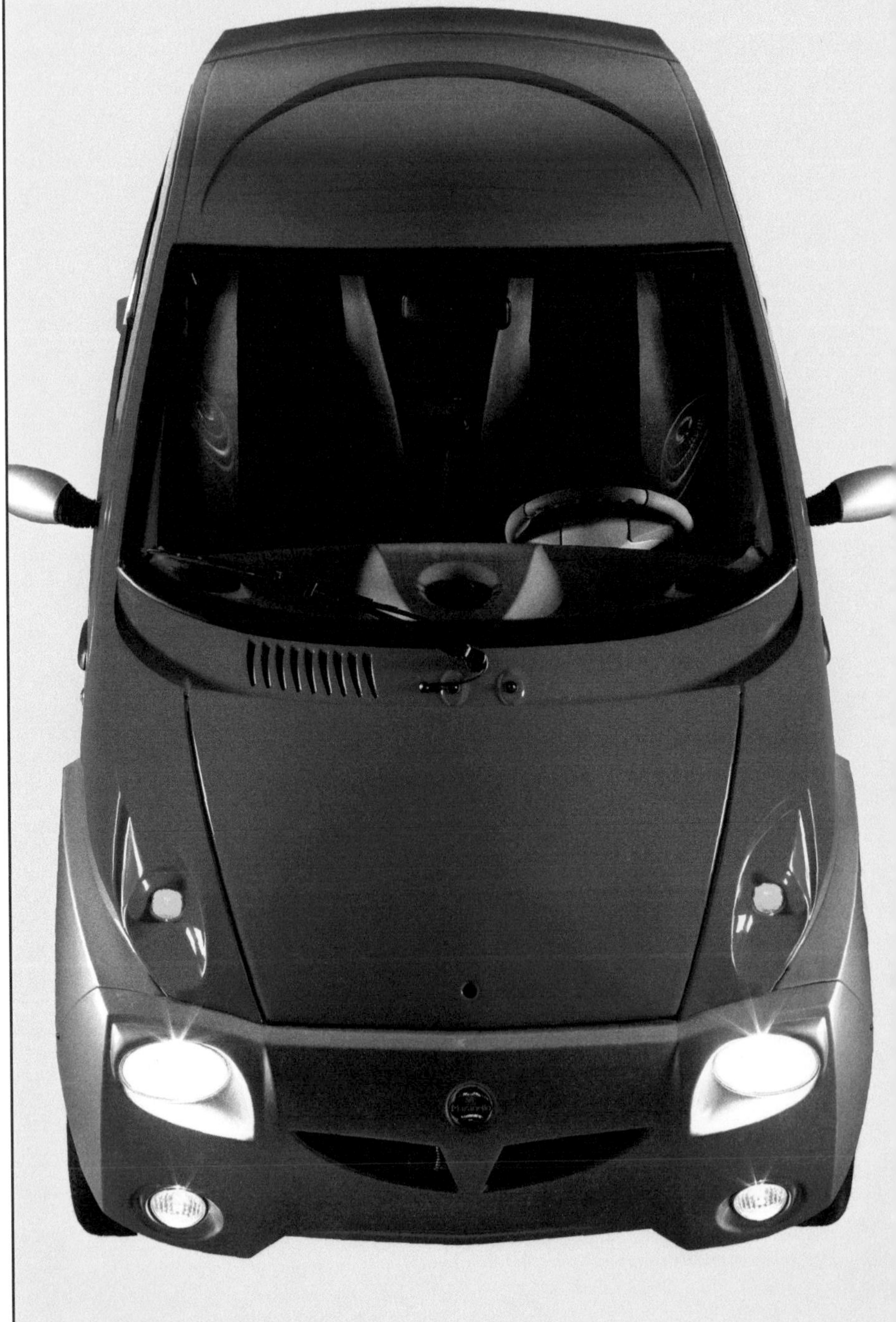

Even though it's fuel free (you just plug it in to a socket in the wall) the reason that the Maranello 4 is catching on, according to Dan (the UK distributor who's also responsible for converting the Maranello 4 into an electric car) is because it makes it's cheap.

"In my experience no one is going to buy a car just because it's green. It has to make total economic sense to them and the Maranello 4 is a no-brainer. It's ideal for people living in London because it's electric and so exempt from road tax, exempt from the congestion charge, and exempt from parking fees in various parts of the city. A doctor who lives in Hampstead bought one this week. He drives to work in Harley Street every day so his tax, parking charges and fuel cost him £5,000 a year. The Maranello costs almost ten grand but in two years he'll have got his money's worth in saved expenses. After that the only outlay will be the annual service charge which is around £150, and an occasional brush replacement."

It's the first day of the World Cup. Scorchingly hot and with a couple of hours to go before the game begins the Kilburn traffic is stuffed with fans trying to get to their mates in time to watch England v Paraguay. Some people look at the car with interest but no one actually seems to be openly laughing about it which surprised me because it looks akin to a Kinder Egg toy.

"Look at that bloke," says Dan, gesturing towards a big dude in a big BMW. "That car must have cost him fifty grand, but is he getting anywhere quicker than us?" To prove it he sneaks us in through a gap in the traffic and we leave the BMW way behind. "If you can afford to have a car like a BMW you can afford to have a car like the Maranello 4 for London driving but still keep the big car for weekend country jaunts or the serious business meetings where you have to impress."

I point out gently that the big dude's car probably wouldn't want a Maranello 4 because the BMW is

SOME PEOPLE LOOK AT THE CAR WITH INTEREST BUT NO ONE ACTUALLY SEEMS TO BE OPENLY LAUGHING ABOUT IT WHICH SURPRISED ME BECAUSE IT LOOKS AKIN TO A KINDER EGG TOY.

"KIDS CAN DRIVE THEM BECAUSE THE CAR IS SO SIMPLE"

a mean machine whereas the Maranello 4 couldn't exactly be described as a car that pulls the birds.

"Depends on the birds," says Dan. "You don't have to be licensed in Europe to drive an electric car so if you're a 14 year old kid in Rome whose Dad is rich enough to buy you one of these to drive yourself to and from school then you and your Dad are probably not having much problem getting the ladies. It beats a lift on a Vespa.

"And kids can drive them because the car is so simple because it's electric. The gears are forwards, backwards. That's it. All you have to do is push the pedals and steer."

The idea of a car that kids can drive on public roads is appropriate because being in the Maranello 4 feels exactly like being in a toy car. You know how, when you're a kid, you look at the dashboard of the car you're playing with and the manufacturer has given you just enough details and stuck just enough tiny speedometer and mileometer stickers to keep you happy? Well, it's like that. There's just about enough controls to convince you that it's a car. But despite the fact that it's smaller than a smart car, it feels just as spacious.

"We got a six foot Sikh and his turban in here the other day with plenty of room left over," says Dan. "You could definitely get a great dane in the back." This is true. Behind us is a boot that sort of sinks down behind into a big basin, big enough to hold a family's weekly shopping.

As we drive up towards home Dan tells me that BMW are working on an electric car that can go at 100mph and I have a sudden vision of what the world would be like in century's time, where only the élite will get the chance to drive a petrol driven car on dedicated tracks or on their private estates. The rest of us will be probably be driving electric or solar panelled vehicles.

And so for those living next to a road the steady drone of the petrol powered car, which once replaced the rifle-shot crack of horses, hooves and cart wheels on cobble stones, will be replaced by a high pitched whine of the electric engine which, judging by the Maranello 4, sounds as aggravating as a mosquito lost in your Eustachian tube. Like anything I guess you'd get used to it but somehow it's sad to think our grand-children may never know the excitement of sitting in a petrol-fuelled sports car, its engine purring and gurgling as it noses it's way up Park Lane or around country roads. But sadder still if they haven't got a planet to drive it on. 🐚

The Sakura Battery Co. Ltd
020 8896 1133 www.sbsbsb.com

"WE GOT A SIX FOOT SIKH AND HIS TURBAN IN HERE THE OTHER DAY WITH PLENTY OF ROOM LEFT OVER."

A RADICAL LIFE

Farmer, journalist, politician, enemy of oppression and friend of the people, William Cobbett's work is as relevant as ever, says John Michell

The Life And Adventures of William Cobbett by Richard Ingrams, Harper Collins, £20.

The *Private Eye* of its time (1802-1835) was Cobbett's *Political Register*, a scandal-raking, racket-busting weekly journal, founded, edited and largely written by the redoubtable William Cobbett, one of the most outstanding characters in English history. He was a Surrey farmer's boy, unschooled but highly self-educated, who thrust his way into politics as a reforming radical and infuriated successive governments by exposing the crooks and racketeers among them. It was not just individuals he denounced but the entire, corrupt system of money-based economics which, he saw, was draining the natural wealth of England from the villages and counties into the great city "wens" of banking and commerce. The modern world

was coming in and Cobbett was appalled by it. A generation earlier, Oliver Goldsmith's poem, "The Deserted Village", had depicted the sad state of rural life, once idyllic but now impoverished by the dominance of urban money. "Ill fares the land, to hastening ills a prey, Where wealth accumulates, and men decay". Cobbett loved that poem, learnt it by heart and assimilated Goldsmith's vision. He too was a poet, not a versifier but a master of the English language in all its modes, from political and personal invective to lyrical descriptions of the English countryside and the beauty of the old way of life that was then passing.

He was a popular writer in his own time—the *Political Register* had a large circulation among all classes, as did the other journals and newspapers he started—while several of the books he wrote were best-sellers and have been published and admired ever since. The most famous of them is Cobbett's *Rural Rides*, a compilation of notes on his journeys through the fields and villages of southern England, and another lasting favourite is his *History of the Protestant Reformation*. This, like all Cobbett's publications, was written for a didactic purpose, to show how drastically the prosperity and native cultures of England and Ireland had been reduced by the centralizing policies of "that old wife-killer", Henry VIII. By robbing the Church of its lands and suppressing the religious institutions that formerly managed them to the benefit

HE WAS A LARGE,
HANDSOME,
ATHLETIC FELLOW,
DELIGHTFUL
COMPANY, A GOOD
HUSBAND AND
FAMILY MAN,
GENEROUS AND
HOSPITABLE IN
THE OLD ENGLISH
STYLE

of the local communities, the Reformation had laid waste the village economy and decimated the rural population. Riding through places that consisted of a few wretched hovels and a few dozen dispirited inhabitants, Cobbett would note the size and fine craftsmanship of their medieval church, built to hold an original population of several hundred independent land-holders. Looking further back, he observed the cultivation terraces that an evidently vast number of prehistoric countrymen had carved into the slopes of the chalk downs. The process of rural decline, he concluded, had been going on for a long time, but the pace of it was rapidly increasing; and unless something were done about it, immediately, the entire fabric of old England—its fine traditions and the high spirit of its people— would disappear for ever. As Goldsmith put it: "... a bold peasantry, their country's pride/ When once destroy'd can never be supplied".

Cobbet could not help doing something about it. As champion of the English people against their ruling oppressors, he was uniquely qualified in every way—through his peasant birth and upbringing; his amazing energy and appetite for learning; his ability to master any subject and clarify its principles; his powerful oratory, loud and outspoken but never coarse, and his total, incorruptible honesty. In person, he was a large, handsome, athletic fellow, delightful company, a good husband and family man, generous and hospitable in the old English style. Throughout his life he worked his own farm. His campaign for the redemption of his country combined the two levels on which he personally operated—the local, practical level of rural affairs and that of national politics at the heart of the realm. On the humble level, Cobbett was determined, by his writings and personal example, to re-educate the rural populace, to restore their culture, to show them how to live independently through their crafts and produce: how to keep bees, grow corn, make straw hats, speak and write grammatically and conduct themselves in ways likely to bring happiness and prosperity. On these and many other subjects he wrote edifying treatises, and with his instructions came prohibitions, such as his blasts against tea-drinking, the cultivation of potatoes and the new vulgar habit of dining in a separate room rather than around the kitchen table. Yet a rural renaissance, as Cobbett soon understood, was not enough. The ultimate cause of degeneration was not local but centred in the nation's capital. London was the place where it had to be fought, so Cobbett extendeed his campaign to Westminster and gained election to Parliament.

His life's work, you could say, ended in failure. The Thing (Cobbett's name for centralized power, big business and finance) has gone from strength to strength and is now the almost unchallenged ruler of not onlyBritain, but the whole world. Cobbett, like most other prophets, expected the imminent collapse of the system he railed against, but instead it has expanded further than he could ever have imagined. There has been continued opposition to this process—by rural revivalists, arts and crafts movements and more recently the ecologists and Green campaigners. Among most of these Cobbett's influence is barely apparent. He was the idealistic type properly called "radical-traditionalist" because his radical opposition to the ruling tendency was in the service of traditional values and culture. The PC culture of today, its urban sentimentality, its effeminacy and the rootless, secular way of thinking that dominates it, would have horrified him. True followers of Cobbett are scarcely heard from these days—with one notable exception, Richard Ingrams. Like many of us he delights in Cobbett's writings, but he has gone farther than anyone in following his footsteps. His *Private Eye* is the direct successor to Cobbett's *Political Register*, neither left nor right in its sympathies, lampooning pretentious idiots and scoundrels of all parties and looking kindly upon the victims of official injustice. In this new biography, *The Life and Adventures of William Cobbett*, Ingrams gives a full, factual and scrupulously fair account of the man; and since he is a witty writer, and you can hardly read about Cobbett without laughing, the result is highly entertaining, sometimes hilarious. This is a very perceptive description of a most worthy and most remarkable character.

STROLLING PLAYER

Michael Smith is a lazy beat poet for the modern age, says Clare Pollard

The Giro Playboy
by Michael Smith,
Faber & Faber, £9.99

The most famous spokesman for the Beat generation, Jack Kerouac, was always a shirker. During his time in the navy he found that going to the doctor with headaches meant he was excused from dull chores, and the authorities noted his "unresponsiveness" to discipline. In later life he gave up on normal jobs, instead hitching round America with his muse Neal Cassady—a man who always said "you gotta go"—on a restless quest that would form the basis of his most famous novel, *On The Road*. An exception was made, on the suggestion of Gary Snyder, for a summer as a fire-lookout in the mountains, where Kerouac would sit endlessly doing nothing, attempting to reach some kind of Zen state of mind.

To be "beat" meant to be exhausted or broke in street slang, but was also—Kerouac later suggested—the beat in "beatific", suggesting epiphany. And now there is a new writer staking a claim to this state of being. Michael Smith's novel *The Giro Playboy* is pitched by Faber as a "twenty-first-century beat classic in the making", and the influence is certainly visible. It recounts the picaresque adventures of a man who is exhausted, broke, and reluctant to opt in to the world of work. Like the Beats watching for fire in the mountains, Smith memorably paints a winter in an out-of-season seaside town as "some kind of religious ordeal". Epiphanies lie everywhere—in scrambled egg that is "like eating a little bit of springtime sun",

cherry blossom in the drains, cranes swaying in the sunset. And as in Kerouac's novels, this is a "fiction" that flirts with memoir—the temptation is always to imagine that the Playboy is Smith himself, and to speculate on the text's closeness to reality (especially as, along with his accompanist Flora, Smith has long performed as "The Giro Playboy"). But if *On The Road* can sometimes seem a little energetic, then this is a beat literature for idlers, a road trip through modern England at a truly leisurely pace. A return ticket to the end of the 242 bus route, rather than a quest for the next thrill in a fast car.

Smith lightly points out his debt to the Beats, in his use of the ellipsis (…) to mark shifts of tone or thought, and most enjoyably in the little poems that parody their eastern-inflected verse - the haiku-like:

Blank pleasant Saturday
drifting round the shops
seemed happy enough

or the more philosophical:

THE BOOK IS PACKED WITH REVERIES... IT IS A JOURNAL OF STROLLS

The moon was in Scorpio
and I was in Tesco
1 frozen pizza
1 pint of milk
1 Terry's Orange
was the mystic result.

However, this is not to agree with the blurb that Smith has quite written a Beat classic yet—and to suggest so seems to be taking this playful book far too seriously. Rather, Smith is sending up his own chosen genre, and having some fun with the icons of cult or underground literature even as he is inspired by their philosophy.

Rimbaud and Baudelaire are also tipped a wink, and the book is packed with druggy reveries (the funniest when he cashes his giro after a particularly tough afternoon at Whitechapel Job Centre and gets "goosed on a bottle of rose and six co-proxamol"). It is also a journal of strolls. The Playboy is a flâneur, who between his doomed and brief attempts at work, spends whole days "circumnavigating London Fields to Stokey on £1.50... looking at all them cows' hooves and chicken claws in the shanty town shacks of Ridley Road Market happy as Larry on two bags of Space Raiders and a Wham Bar". I live near this market, and we're really not talking a very large area. In another century he would surely, like the wanderers of Paris, have walked with a pet tortoise to set a dawdling pace. Intriguingly, whilst the book is cunningly disguised as a novel, it is truly a series of experiments in that most French of forms, the prose poem. Most of the "paragraphs" would stand alone, and are dense with rhythm and image. Whilst, understandably, Smith's editor has decided to reach the widest audience by assembling these into a narrative, perhaps Smith's most interesting selling point is that he has finally found an English voice for this Baudelairean form.

Judged as a novel, on the other hand, it may disappoint certain readers who are used to "page-

THE GIRO PLAYBOY

by Michael Smith

'Like Rimbaud on the dole.' Tom Hodgkinson, *The Idler*

ff

AT THE CENTRE OF
THE BOOK IS THE
STORY OF A MAN'S
BATTLE AGAINST
THE WORLD OF
WORK

turners", with its lack of momentum—epiphanies lead nowhere, and although the character has to make a decision by the end of the book, many of his wanderings are down dead ends. More positively, this means the book is also that thing of great pleasure to idle readers—one that can simply be dipped into. Smith excels at moments, and has a gift for evoking place that can conjure a world in a single line. He begins with a delightfully shabby Brighton, with its: "Clotted cream Regency houses dreaming of themselves... the fairylights twinkling along the prom in the evening... the 24-hour gay greasy spoons." Later we get trips to the North East "where women on crutches wait in bus queues that last a long time", and into "six-toed Essex... the scary badlands of the crazed backwoodsman". Better yet are his descriptions of a particular cultural moment though—the Shoreditch/Hoxton phenomenon of the late 1990s.

Nowadays it seems increasingly fashionable to sneer at Hoxton as a kind of nexus of Nathan (and Natalie) Barleys; all sniggering rich kids in pork-pie hats and fingerless gloves—and there is, of course, some truth in this. But it should also be remembered that its slightly grotesque "trendiness" arose because a bunch of talented and idealistic young people decided to create an artistic community, bringing with them a taste for retro, craft, theatricality and DIY. When I first arrived in London and moved to a house off Brick Lane, I could hardly believe there was a huge area right next to the city that contained no All Bar Ones or Starbucks or Carphone Warehouses. Instead there were strange little galleries, shops selling handmade plastic jewellery and legwarmers, Gilbert and George walking past in unison, Banksys on the walls, and cafés full of knackered old furniture and free 'zines and girls whizzing up smoothies in full 1950s glamour-outfits. On a weekend in Hoxton you might see a little fête set up with bunting, cake stalls and artists running tombolas; or be flyered for a tea dance or burlesque show; or find

Tracey Emin dancing on the table next to you. The people, I might also add, tended to be very young and beautiful, and often wear strange earrings or garish socks, and have asymmetrical haircuts. And maybe that makes them wankers, but then the people who say that probably spend their weekends drinking Magners in Gap chinos, so who's the wanker really? I mean, at least these kids weren't bland...

Anyway, as Smith observes, the area is now fighting creeping gentrification—"all sanitised water features and silver birches and city women driving around in Smart cars"—and so it's a pleasure to find someone capturing the Hoxton of a few years ago so memorably. Smith thrusts the Playboy into a job at Shoreditch institution "The Pub" (which illustrations suggest to be The Bricklayer's Arms), and likens it to "being a yellow coat at some demented resort". From this vantage point he takes us on a carnivalesque trip through the area's private views and parties. Whilst aware of the silliness of it all—"stylists and fashion PRs who dressed like Kajagoogoo; Japanese photo shoots down the back alley"—the Playboy also captures the sense of glee and possibility of a time when a place "a stone's throw from the grind of the global financial zone, seemed to be gathering together another kind of England, and its shanty backstreets and tenements became the open and welcoming refuge of England's dreaming..."

For idlers though, the real meat of the book —and what makes it so refreshing—is that at its centre is the story of a man's battle against the world of work. The Playboy tries various jobs, but they always fail to provide him with purpose, happiness or enough money for it to seem a fair exchange for his time. On the lowest rung of the corporate ladder, in a building with "acrylic odours" and "a moronic toytown quality", he is finally driven to quit by corporate Christmas cards, and the fact he can "see right through it"—a queasy sensation most of us have experienced at some time. But menial

jobs turn out to be no nobler, and eventually even getting up at "Z o'clock" on his "giro holiday" starts to feel demeaning and dull—particularly because of the grinding poverty that this involves, reducing him to: "slying round the aisles of Sainsburys, eating all their croissants as a free lunch."

For all the knowing cool and nods to cult fiction that suffuse this novel, at the heart of it is a character who is 'bored bored BORED. And as his adventures progress we get the sinking feeling that—despite its small victories and weird glamour—this is no way to live. Eventually, the Playboy realises that idleness is not the same as laziness, and a serious illness convinces him that if he wants a magical life, he has to stop waiting for little scraps of magic to come to him, and instead go out and grab them. He immerses himself in his writing because: "Art, like cricket or cooking or doing the garden, is work as pleasure, work as play, which is the only thing I could imagine myself being any good at." It is a wise and hard-won conclusion, and one can only hope that Smith will follow his protagonist's lead, and go on being good at it for a long time. ◉

BOOKS

WOLF SOLENT

Tony White on a classic from the under-appreciated John Cowper Powys

John Cowper Powys (1872-1963) is today a vastly unfashionable English novelist, largely forgotten. His masterpiece, *Wolf Solent*, is hard to find, but there are still a few copies of Penguin's "modern classics" edition of 2000 to be had out there, and it's well worth hunting out any edition of it that you can find.

Published in 1929, the novel tells the story of its eponymous protagonist, who returns to his family's roots in Dorset to take up the job of research assistant to a malevolent local squire who is intent on writing a scurrilous history of the county. Solent's own family, too, is not without its scandals, and his dead father's skeleton, rotting as it is in the Dorset soil (rather than any cupboard), is practically a character in the novel.

Solent himself is a sensitive near-visionary with a habit, from childhood, of willing himself into mystical states of consciousness—"sinking into his soul"—during which he imagines himself at one with the teeming life surrounding him. We're introduced to this mysticism at the very beginning of the book, as he travels down from Waterloo and, accompanied as it is by extravagantly detailed descriptions of "the extraordinary variety of organic patterns in the roots and twigs and land-plants and water-plants", the reader is quickly seduced into an empathy with Solent's seeking after sensation, and Powys's summoning of a countryside in which the thrill of every reed or leaf is significant. It would, of course, be anachronistic to call this vivid summoning of nature "trippy", but it's perhaps understandable that he was last in something approaching favour during the pre-punk 1970s. Testament to this is the hippy dippy Glastonbury-kitsch cover of Picador's now out of print edition of his even more massive novel, *A Glastonbury Romance*. That was printed in 1975, not so long, but then again an age, before their 1984 publication of Kathy Acker's *Blood and Guts in High School Plus Two* allowed them to re-brand themselves for a young, post-punk generation (including me and my friends) who were eager to find the contemporary successors to purveyors of literary experiment (teenage kicks) like Burroughs, Ballard, Moorcock et al.

In his introduction to the 3AM webzine's new anthology of short fiction and essays, *The Edgier Waters*, Michael Bracewell marks the early 1980s as the moment when the UK publication of Kathy Acker "introduced younger British writers (and

HAVING READ THIS NOVEL, IT'S HARD TO LOOK AT THE SOUTH WEST OF ENGLAND IN THE SAME WAY AGAIN

publishers) to the idea that there could possibly be a connection between the people who bought interesting records ... and the people who bought interesting books." This was a connection that Picador seemed to exploit for a few short years in the 1980s, not least by enlisting a new wave of jacket designers from the record industry, like Vaughan Oliver and Nigel Grierson's 23 Envelope, now V23. Unfortunately *A Glastonbury Romance* didn't benefit from this new kind of marketing.

I first read a battered copy of Wolf Solent back in the summer of 1997. Hot days spent lounging around the vast West End flat I was house-sitting were given substance by Solent's Dorset-bound rambles, and his far from straightforward love affairs with two local girls, Gerda and Christie. And while his mysticism partly fuels the complications of his love life, it also grounds him: "So indifferent to all human fates did he feel just then, that... he gave himself up to a physical sensation of being an integral portion of this wide, somnolent landscape! 'I am Poll's Camp,' he would have said, if the sensation had articulated itself. 'I am Lovelace Park. I am the Gwent Lanes. I am Nevilton Hill. I am Melbury Bub. I am Blackmore Vale and High Stoy. It is over me that Gerda and Lob are now walking down there by the Lunt.'"

Having read this novel, it's hard to look at the south west of England in the same way again. That view from the train window in the opening chapter of *Wolf Solent*, which could just as easily slip unnoticed past the contemporary traveller, becomes, thanks to Powys, dramatic in the extreme. As Berkshire and then Wiltshire give way to Dorset and Somerset, the landscape does markedly change beneath those big Atlantic skies. Glastonbury Tor slips past to the north and the gentle fields and hills give way to something altogether darker and in thrall to a kind of hyper-fecundity, which sees trees and hedges so overburdened with foliage and creepers that they almost appear to be rotting on the branch. Here the tight aerobatic flying of high-tech fighter aircraft—their close diamond formations whipping from one horizon to the other—seems as fundamentally a part of nature as birdsong.

In his 1916 volume *One Hundred Best Books* (which is preserved, free, online by the Project Gutenberg web archive), John Cowper Powys ponders, "the advice to be given to young and ardent people, in the matter of their reading..." He rails paradoxically against the "reading list", against the idea of a literary canon and its companion notion (a "vice" no less) that reading could be seen as a path to wisdom or learning. Instead he argues for the importance of imagination ("With imagination to help us we can make something of our days"), and the way that reading purely for pleasure can occasionally give us a breath of some greater wind. He sings the praises of those idlers who "in the old sweet epicurean way, loved to loiter through huge digressive books, with the ample unpremeditated enjoyment of leisurely travellers wayfaring along a wonderful road." This essay is more than just a gentle rant against forced education or self-improvement however, it can also be read as a statement of intent—and Wolf Solent is the richest, most delightful fruition of this manifesto. ☺

Further reading

Kathy Acker, *Blood and Guts in High School Plus Two*, Picador.

John Cowper Powys, *Wolf Solent*, Penguin Modern Classics, £14.99

Andrew Stevens (ed), *The Edgier Waters: New Writing from Literary Upstarts*, Snow Books, £7.99

Vaughan Oliver and V23 Poster Designs, V23 (distributed by www.artbooks.de) Euros 39.00

BOOKSHELF
IAIN SINCLAIR

Photographed by Tony White

NOTHING REALLY MATTERS

Author Tom Lutz talks to Sabine Steinlein about 400 years of slacker culture

L utz is sort of a slacker specialist. Inspired by his couch-surfing son Cody, he investigated the leisurely life in *Doing Nothing – A History of Loafers, Loungers, Slackers, and Bums in America* (published by Farrar, Straus and Giroux, June 2006). *Doing Nothing* examines the conflicts people who refuse to work face and the impact they have on others. To Lutz the slacker is "a critique of our culture's twisty relation to work and to leisure." The slacker serves as a lens through which he inspects the work ethics and work environment of his particular time.

Among the scores of workless –Lutz's bibliography spans well over 500 entries—are figures from literature, film, television and reality. Tearing through Lutz's book I encountered Bartleby, The Scrivener, whose famous sentence "I would prefer not to" drove his boss from his Wall Street office. I ran into Goethe's Werther, Goncharov's Oblomov, Bertrand Russell, Paul Lafargue and Jack Kerouac (a writer too lazy to edit his own prose). I also learned that these "lazy" guys weren't called slackers back then: The term "slacker" was originally used to label those who dodged World War I. (Various propaganda movies from the time carry the term "Slacker" in their titles.)

This notion leads Lutz to the draft-dodging, vacation-loving US President. "George W. Bush," Lutz writes, "will likely go down in history as our slacker president." No slacker can flee Lutz's reach. The author travels as far as to Japan to meet the free-tah, the contemporary Japanese slacker. The last four hundred centuries of loafing and sauntering make for a riveting reading experience.

IDLER: Mr. Lutz, in your book you explore the last three or four centuries of American and European slacker culture. Can you give a couple of examples as to how the slacker has changed according to his or her time in history?

LUTZ: Whenever the world of work changes, the slacker figure appear on the cultural horizon. At each point, the slacker figure takes on some of the other cultural issues that are involved in the changing work place. So when Joseph Dennie, an early American slacker, writes up his slacker figures in the late 18th and early 19th centuries he pretends to have aristocratic sentiments, attitudes and predilections, but, in fact, he was a middle class person himself. The change seemed to

ANNE FISHBEIN

be a change from a world in which the aristocracy
ran things to a world in which the manufacturing
elite ran things. So the slacker figure then had an
aristocratic quality, a quality which was passing.
When Jack Kerouac came on the scene in the
middle of the 20th century, he affected a working
class image because older working class values
seemed to have been lost: the world of work
changed into one in which people were shuffling
papers in office buildings rather than actually
making things. So the Beats wore blue jeans, work
boots and t-shirts, the clothes of the working class.
But there is no even line of development. At each
point it's a very specific flavour related to the other

> "IN MY OWN LIFE
> THERE HAVE
> BEEN MOMENTS
> IN WHICH I HAVE
> DECIDED THAT I
> DID NOT HAVE TO
> HAVE A CAREER"

issues.

IDLER: How would you define the contemporary slacker?

LUTZ: When people think about the contemporary slacker, they often think of the activities the slacker takes part in. That means sitting on the couch watching TV, playing videogames or spending all their time on the computer. So more than a dress style or a relation to a certain class, contemporary slackers are defined by their relation to the media. The Beats, the American expatriates in the 1920s or the Jazz Age slackers were defined by drinking, drugs or poetry, not in relation to the mass media and media games, which is what the contemporary slacker is all about.

IDLER: To me it seems, to a certain extent, the slacker is defined by the perception of others...

LUTZ: Yes, to some extent the slacker is always in the eye of the beholder. In my own life there have been moments in which I decided that I did not have to have a career. It was an ethical decision against ruining the planet. But there are also times when I cannot seem to do anything except play a game on my computer, and I berate myself for being a slacker. There's no ethical force to it at all, it's simply my own procrastination. And then there are times when people think, "Wow, you don't really ever work. You have to go to your teaching job once or twice a week and that's not a real job. You are really a slacker." Of course, I don't feel like that about myself. Most of the time, I feel like I work fairly hard.

IDLER: Do you think slackers ever suffer from their slacking?

LUTZ: It might be impossible to be countercultural without suffering. If you are not a sociopath, you feel social pressure to conform. If you decide not to conform, there is going to be a certain amount of suffering. The adoption of a counter- or sub-cultural identity may be a way to alleviate suffering. Or it may increase your suffering. It can change by

the moment, depending on who you are with or who you are imagining you are with.

IDLER: I noticed that the media's attention has recently shifted to the slacker. Steve McKevitt's book "City Slackers" just came out, and there have been a number American guide books that advice people on how to appear busy at work while actually slacking. Is there a trend?

LUTZ: Yes, I think there is a little bubble of slacker figures right now. It has to do with the outsourcing of various jobs. So there is an anxiety about the future of work and that's always one of the prime ingredients for the flourishing of such cultural representations.

IDLER: Many of the slackers in your book are also writers. Do you think there is a correlation between slacking and writing?

LUTZ: We know about the slacker because of writers. So to a certain extent, the writer has created the slackers. And then, there is something about

PIONEERS OF SLACKING.
LEFT: WALT WHITMAN
RIGHT: JOSEPH DENNIE

"I REALLY STILL EMBRACE FIGHTING WHAT'S WRONG IN THE CULTURE"

the nature of that activity: writing is often difficult for the outside to understand. If you see somebody nailing two boards together you see them working. If you see somebody farming a field, you see them working. And when you see somebody writing you just see them sitting in a chair. It just doesn't look like work. It doesn't even look like work to the person who is doing it. Writing includes an enormous amount of time reading, sauntering, sitting, thinking and doing all sorts of things that people don't associate with work.

IDLER: So doing nothing is part of the creative process?

LUTZ: Yes, and looking like you are doing nothing is even a greater part of the creative process. Your work is somebody else's recreation. People doodle when they are not doing anything. They draw, they play music. So writing doesn't look like work to them. That's why sports and Hip Hop figures often seem like slackers, no matter how much actual work is involved.

IDLER: But that means that the line between the slacker and the worker is very hard to draw.

LUTZ: Mihaly Csikszentmihalyi talks about "flow," the psychology of engagement with everyday life. Creativity is having a sense of flow. When we're enjoying our work, it's because we're in this sense of flow. You could argue that when you are in a reverie lying on your back in a field watching the clouds go by, that's a certain kind of flow as well. So slacking, creativity and being one with one's work have a lot of common ground.

IDLER: Can "slacker" even be a category, considering that the term is so malleable and mostly a matter of perspective?

LUTZ: Richard Linklater, who made the film "Slacker," said that he and his friends were using the term in the same way gay people adopted "queer": taking a derogatory comment, owning it and resisting the meanings of that derogatory term in the culture. But since it's meant to be

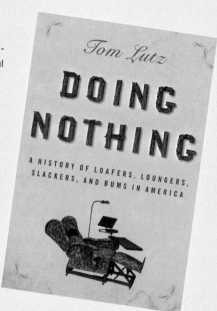

derogatory, adopting it as a form of self-derision maybe is not particularly helpful for anybody.

It may be that the term slacker itself is on the cusp of being replaced, that we're at the tail end of the usefulness of slacker as a term. The same way "loafer" and "lounger" dropped out of common usage.

IDLER: What qualities in slackers do you personally like?

LUTZ: What am I doing right now? I'm talking to you. Am I working or am I slacking off? There's ways in which I still enjoy those moments. I feel like somehow I'm being a slacker. I really still embrace fighting what's wrong in the culture. Or the feeling that having become a workaholic, I've made a mistake. I feel pleasure when I see people get away with things. I want the thief to get away with it. There's something about the love of the outlaw that's part of it, about that American love of getting something for nothing.

IDLER: And which qualities do you resent?

LUTZ: I was working at an art school last year and a couple of people on my faculty didn't do their jobs. They were slackers! If they had an option to do something or not do it, they would always choose not to do it. Those moments where somebody else's slacking makes more work for you, those are moments where you resent the slacker.

IDLER: How is your son Cody? Still on your couch?

LUTZ: He's fine. He's a writer as well. So he faces some of the same problems that you and I face, which is that sometimes it's hard to work and sometimes there's no way of measuring our output very effectively. He's a smart guy and he knows that being a slacker was a moment in his life and that it is also an ongoing issue. It will be for him as it is for all of us. 🔘

EASY SOUNDS

PROFILE: SHIRLEY COLLINS

Will Hodgkinson goes down to Lewes to meet the grand lady of folk

How do you inhabit a song that you didn't write? If you want to know, listen to *Love, Death And The Lady* by Shirley and Dolly Collins. Featuring sparse, cold, almost monastic piano, harpsichord, sackbut and lute arrangements by her sister Dolly, Shirley Collins sings traditional working class British folk songs, all centuries old and none of them authored, with such stark tragedy that you are convinced she must be singing about her own life. "As I walked out one morn in May, the birds did sing and the lambs did play," begins the opening track, *Death And The Lady*, sounding more like a medieval funeral procession than a celebration of summer. "I met an old man by the way." This is the introduction to one of the most personal, tender and bleak albums of the 1970s, featuring songs that have their resonance from being shared and passed down over centuries.

Love, Death And The Lady is about death, sex, violence, isolation and loneliness. In "The Oxford Girl", the singer tells of his murder of a lover in a jealous

rage ("I plucked a stick from out of the hedge and I gently knocked her down"). In "Are You Going To Leave Me?" Shirley Collins contains her passionate despair under a cloak of British dignity as she sounds reconciled to her encroaching misery. As for "Young Girl Cut Down In Her Prime", it's best not to even go there if you're feeling at all sensitive. This is music from the bottom of a deep well of experience, although none of the words that Shirley Collins sings are her own.

Shirley Collins recorded *Love, Death And The Lady* in 1970. She was splitting up with her husband, looking after two young children at her home in Blackheath, southeast London and facing a bleak future. Despite being hailed as the queen of the English folk scene—her pure, unadorned voice had brought depth to traditional songs on the 1965 album *Folk Roots, New Routes* (with the guitarist Davy Graham) and the 1969 medieval classic *Anthems In Eden*, which paved the way for Fairport Convention and the British folk-rock movement —impeccable credentials did not translate to album sales. Shirley was broke and lonely.

I'm from the generation that believes good singers write their own material. The Beatles, The Rolling Stones, Bob Dylan and The Velvet Underground set the standard for critically acclaimed rock bands to write what they play, and I'm sure that had I heard her as a teenager Shirley Collins would have meant nothing to me, just as traditional music as a whole was something I viewed as rather stiff. The whole concept of serving a song that you didn't write was alien. But

when I came to *Love, Death And The Lady*, well into adulthood, it knocked me for six.

I became so deeply involved in *Love, Death And The Lady* that I felt I had to meet its singer. Shirley Collins was not hard to find—she lives by herself in Lewes, East Sussex, in a pretty stone cottage near the castle, where she tends to her overcrowded garden, receives her grandchildren (she was born in 1935) and deals with an ever-increasing amount of interest in her past work and life following the 2005 publication of *America Over The Water*, her memoir of travelling across America to collect folk songs, aged 20, with her then-boyfriend the American archivist Alan Lomax. Conversations with Shirley over the course of arranging the interview put me in mind of a sweet-natured granny—"I'll make us a light lunch, dear, and we can talk over that"—but the reality is a lot more complex.

SHIRLEY COLLINS AND BANJO, CIRCA 1964

"THESE ARE SONGS
THAT DEAL WITH
UNIVERSAL THEMES
AND STORIES AND
THEY DO FOR YOU
WHAT YOU NEED
THEM TO DO"

As she brought me a coffee and drank one herself from a large brown clay mug with "Shirley" sculpted onto the side of it, I asked her how she could put herself so deeply into songs that someone else wrote. "It's not that someone else wrote them," she said, with a hint of admonishment. "It's that 1,000 other people have sung them and shared that experience. These are songs that deal with universal themes and stories and they do for you what you need them to do. I always believe that when you sing a folk song, it is not yours, and that when I sing I stand slightly outside of it while also being totally involved. I'm a conduit for all of this stuff that has gone on before me."

While folk music is often defined by a certain mood or style, Shirley Collins sees it as strictly the preserve of the traditional, usually anonymous songs, in which authorship is not really an issue but the shared experience that the history of the song contains is. "I do quite like Neil Young, and I think "The Night They Drove Old Dixie Down" by The Band is wonderful, but they don't talk to me or reach me in the way the old songs do. I think I'm a throwback anyway, which is daft because I enjoy living in the modern world in 2006, but some cast in my mind forces me to go back to older things. I don't listen to much music after Handel. The old songs say everything I could possibly want to say."

A few years ago I bought an album Shirley made in 1960, aged 21, called *False True Lovers*. It has nothing of the feeling of *Love, Death And The Lady* and puts me in mind of the kind of music I associated with folk as a teenager: something rather twee, the concern of a preservation society in provincial England. I told Shirley that I didn't think it was a great album. "How could it be good? What did I know at that age? When I was a child we used to sing a song called "Two Sisters". In the original version one sister is jealous of the other and throws her in the river and drowns her, and then the dead sister is transformed into a lyre

and some musicians play a song on her bones. It goes back to Greek mythology. But at home we sang it as a piece of nonsense. "Hey down, boy down, a farmer lived in the West Country. He had daughters one, two and three, and I'll be true to my love if my love will be true to me. As they were walking by the river's brim, the eldest pushed the youngest in." It ends with the verse: "the eldest she fled across the sea and died a maid among black savagees." On *False True Lovers* I was singing about 'black savagees' because I had no experience of life, and you can hear it in my voice."

A few years later it seemed that she did have some experience. *Folk Routes, New Roots* (1965) is the album with which Shirley Collins announced herself as a major talent and, despite a repertoire consisting only of cover versions, entirely original. On the cover she sits primly in an arts and crafts-style smock, looking rather matronly and old beyond her years, while Davy Graham glowers in the background like a morally questionable gypsy.

At the time Collins was a young mother and the budding rose of the English folk movement, while Davy Graham was busy imitating the bohemian lifestyles of his American jazz musician heroes and nurturing a heroin habit to go with it.

"He was the epitome of elegant guitar playing, an absolutely remarkable musician," said Shirley of Davy. "But he was difficult to work with, especially as I was a young mother with normal, everyday problems. I remember one time he refused

> "ONE TIME DAVY GRAHAM REFUSED TO GET ON THE SAME TRAIN AS ME BECAUSE OF SOME PERCEIVED ARTISTIC DIFFERENCE, WHICH I FOUND VERY OFFENSIVE"

the words. "If all the young men were hares on the mountain, how many young girls would take guns and go hunting?" she sings on "Hares On The Mountain", and the fact that she delivers it so innocently makes it all the more haunting. The darkness of the British folk traditions is encapsulated on Nottamun Town, which mentions stark naked drummers and a company of kings in a way that sounds like a riddle.

"It's an upside-down song," said Shirley of Nottamun Town. "Everything is contrary, which sounds to me like witchcraft but perhaps I'm being fanciful. The lyrics talk of sitting down on a 'hot cold frozen stone', and of getting flung from a horse: 'he bruised my hide and tore my shirt'. In a great song there is always something out of sight, something elusive. And although I like to think about the origins of these songs, the most appealing thing is that none of us really know for sure where they came from; we're just scrabbling around in the dark."

to get on the same train as me because of some perceived artistic difference, which I found very offensive. And he took so many drugs, which I've always hated; I just don't come from the kind of background in which you take drugs. I remember when one of the members of The Incredible String Band said to my sister Dolly: 'You've never seen a tree properly until you've seen it on LSD.' She screamed at him: 'I've seen more trees than you'll see in your entire life!'"

The unlikely pairing made for one of the great albums of the 1960s, in which Davy Graham manages to find the ancient Eastern threads within English folk while Shirley's pure, unadorned voice transmits the mystery and eroticism of

Over the afternoon, Shirley talked about her dislike of religion ("it scares me—you can kill prostitutes or invade countries in the name of God"), her socialist roots, the sanctity of the songs that she has made it her life's work to honour, and her lifelong dislike of pop. "Pop music is generally a background for people to posture over," she said as she put the kettle on for another cup of tea. "When I went to America with Alan Lomax we met blues players like Mississippi Fred McDowell and Muddy Waters. Fred McDowell had been picking cotton the day we met him, and he was in his fifties and had never played outside of his area before, let alone make a recording. When you come back to England after that to hear a band like The Rolling Stones, they just seem like a bunch of silly, preening boys. Fred McDowell had such dignity, even though the songs he sings might be filthy. To me there is nothing worse than ghastly Madonna thrusting her crotch to raise funds for Children In Need on television at six in the evening."

folk
roots,
new
routes
*Shirley
Collins
Davy
Graham*

Shirley Collins' own great tragedy was that she lost her singing voice in the 1980s. She has not performed since. But she has made a handful of albums that have preserved the finest British folk songs with clarity and depth, and *Love, Death And The Lady* is the album that holds her most remarkable moments.

"I was at a low point and I chose songs that reflected my state of mind," said Shirley as she walked me towards Lewes train station before I took the journey back to London. "I had a common

ODD COUPLE: THE MATRONLY SHIRLEY COLLINS WITH THE MORALLY QUESTIONABLE DAVY GRAHAM

feeling with the people in the songs, especially as these stories are couched in such perfect language. But singing traditional music... Christ, it's really been hard-going. It's no wonder most people stick to pop music."

IDLE PURSUITS

PITCH PERFECT

Matthew De Abaitua on the appeal of camping for those in populous city pent.

I have been fulminating against articles in the national press about the cool or contrariwise uncool nature of camping. Those swine spoil everything. No sooner had I finished pegging out my trusty tent than an acre of newsprint blew my way. There I read a backlash piece by Jacques Peretti in the *Guardian* describing the hell of driving to France for a camping holiday on a megasite in Brittany. He was backlashing against a camping fad trailed in the posh papers. Style journalists had rattled on about their friend's yurt, Kate Moss wearing wellies and a Mintel report that noted a small percentage increase in the sales of caravans since 2000. (The maxim of pundit journalism; two of my acquaintances are doing the same thing. Find me a spurious report cooked up by some "experts", get typing and don't spare the zeitgeists.)

This newsprint spat upset me because camping means more to me than just a seasonal fad.

I have taken to it in the same way George W Bush took to Jesus, the second time around. Sure, I camped as a child, back in the 1970s, but it took until fatherhood for me to become a born again camper, a canvas zealot, and no aspect of my being—from my politics to my musical taste—has remained untouched by this pursuit.

When I came across the "cool camping" article, I was pitched beside a turn in Grinds Brook near the village of Edale in the Peak district. Grinds Brook draws its water from tor and moor, spluttering down six hundred metres of valley before trickling through Fieldhead campsite. There, sheep and their lambs nibble dutifully upon its banks. As it was late May, the lambs were larger and more confident than the shivering shanks I had seen up in the Outer Hebrides in Easter. I am beginning to notice these little things, learning the basics of nature after ten years holed up in the inner city.

At Fieldhead, I woke with the dawn chorus. Lying quietly in the tent, I listened to the intricate melodies of the song thrush more intently than ever before. In the city, I don't do dawn, waking late after staying up to midnight watching television, taking in more advertising, attending to the various microtasks of modern husbandry. I don't lie around listening to the birds. Urban birdsong is an abrasive chatter in my back garden. From their roost overlooking the railway station, magpies ask nervous questions of one another in the thunderous wake of a freight train,

conferring on how best to answer the screech of great rusted wheels against the rails. To the automated apologies of the station tannoy, the birds responded with announcements of their own. Their beaks run off monologues like sewing needles pecking thread, imitating ringtone and car alarm alike in the hope of striking up some kind of relationship with the indifferent city. I know that feeling.

What have I been missing all my life? A day, so insignificant in the city, buds, ripens, flowers, wilts and dies while camping, the whole shape of life staged in microcosm. Normally I miss the beginning

CAMPING SLOWS TIME; THIS IS WHY, FOR ALL ITS HARDSHIPS, I SEE IT AS AN IDLE PURSUIT

of this cycle, dawn, and the end too, the dusk, when the daylight is engrained by night and midges drift over the campsite forming patches of interference. To outrun the inevitable night—you sense it hovering, waiting, the reaper itself—wagtails step up their acrobatics, hopscotching over river stones to gather a last supper. Later I will skulk from tent to toilet under a night sky so riddled with stars that I stoop under weight of all that infinity.

Camping slows time; this is why, for all its hardships, I see it as an idle pursuit. It reclaims the intensity of the moment. Every other weekend from the first May Bank Holiday until mid-September, my family and I sleep under polyester and polyethylene. Without a car, we haul ourselves across the public transport system of the British Isles, all we need packed into my eighty litre rucksack until I resemble King Kong's valet.

THE MONTREAL BIOSPHÈRE, R. BUCKMINSTER FULLER'S PRECURSOR TO THE MODERN DOME TENT

For an idler, it sounds like a terrific amount of effort, which it is. The packing alone would

KNIVES AND FIRE —HOW CAN YOU RESIST?

have defeated my younger self. Our clothes are dutifully folded into compression sacks and rolled up tight, all surplus air expelled. The beds squash down into the size of toilet rolls. For illumination, we have the trusty maglite, a torch I first encountered as a security guard, where its heft and girth suggested it could moonlight as a weapon. Also, a handful of lightsticks to take the edge off the night. Lightsticks work by a process called chemoluminescence, in which a chemical reaction produces light, in this case a fluorescent dye triggered by cyalume reacting with hydrogen peroxide. Heat makes the dye brighter and when cool it gives off a dull glow, perfect for a night light for a young child. The sleeping bags crumple satisfying into their sacks—I take pleasure in the way camping demands bags for your bags, it demands a certain anal retentive, organisational sensibility, and I have grown to appreciate this aspect of my character after years of romanticising the more chaotic expressions of the self. For cold nights, I throw in two silk linings, again in their own little bags, each no bigger than a fag packet. When I sleep I am within a bag within a bag within the tent, which has a bag all to itself.

Next come the knives. The Swiss army knife, of course, with its nifty pair of tweezers, necessary for extracting nature's arrows, the ticks, bee stings, thorns and splinters that are a part of any camping trip. I also have an Opinel knife with a beech handle and 12cm stainless steel blade, because I am worth it. Next in goes the Trangia stove, an arrangement of pans, kettle, cooking stand and frying pan stacked one-inside-the-other. The Trangia runs on methylated spirits and so a bottle of that purple-dyed fuel goes in to the bag too. Knives and fire—how can you resist?

The tent itself weighs seven kilos, which is fairly hefty. Machismo wants something smaller, light and hardy, a mountaineering tent perhaps, but these are family trips not an extreme sport. The tunnel tent is very simple to put up, structured around

IN AN AGE OF PLENTY, THERE IS SOMETHING SELF-IMPROVING ABOUT CARRYING ONLY WHAT YOU NEED

three long fibreglass poles. It was the shift from the heavy frame tents with their canvas flysheet and separate plastic groundsheet to the lighter, dome tents that makes car-less camping possible.

The father of the modern tent is R.Buckminster Fuller, a true American visionary. He deplored waste, was concerned with self-sustainability and was on a mission "to find what a single individual can contribute to changing the world and benefiting all humanity."

After the Second World War, Fuller focused on developing shelter designs that were so light, they could be delivered by air. In 1954 he patented the geodesic dome, which adhered to the principle of "doing more with less" by creating the maximum amount of space with the minimum amount of materials. The geodesic dome is half a sphere constructed out of a complex network of triangles. Fuller envisaged this invention as solving a predicted housing crisis. His domestic dome is yet to catch on, yet the dome tent is a ubiquitous sight at festivals and campsites across the world. The development of the lightweight flexible poles, made out of either aluminum or fiberglass, which bend like fresh hazel wood (the natural material used by the Newbury protestors to construct their "bender" structures) made Fuller's invention portable.

In the 1970s, North Face brought a Fuller-inspired tent to market, the "Oval Intention". Invented by Bob Gillis, the early prototype has a canvas cotton exterior hanging over a lattice of bendy poles, with a large oval entrance. Recalling the Pompidou centre in France, with its exteriorized pipes, the poles form an exoskeleton from which the canvas is stung. In 1978, North Face further refined the Oval Intention into the Vector Equilibrium-24, an expedition tent that, in their words, is "the perfect embodiment of R. Buckminster Fuller's theory of sphericity incorporating 'maximum efficiency with minimum materials'".

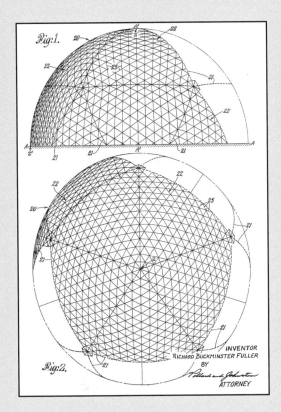

Fig:1.

Fig:2.

INVENTOR
RICHARD BUCKMINSTER FULLER
BY

ATTORNEY

There is concord between Fuller's revulsion toward waste and my delight in bags-within-bags, one-thing-inside-another-inside-another. Camping's frugality of space and resources becomes more appealing as the bric-a-brac of home ownership accumulates. In an age of plenty, there is something self-improving in carrying only what you need, and no more, and leaving no trace behind when you go.

The dome tent superseded the traditional A-frame, which has all but disappeared. The A-frame demanded exact pitching to keep the inner and outer tent separate (contact between the two compromised the surface tension this A-frame relies upon for waterproofing, hence the perennial cry of "don't touch the sides"). Also, as the "A" suggests, the tent narrowed to a peak, meaning it lacked headspace. The refinement of nylon was another vital piece in the creation of the modern tent, as it resulted in a move away from heavy cotton canvas (often waterproofed with wax paraffin, which stank) to a lighter covering.

With its origins in the post-war utopianism of Buckminster Fuller, and its use of modern technology, camping equipment is futuristic

THE RETURN OF CAMPING HAS A WIDER RELEVANCE BEYOND MERELY BEING A NICE WAY TO SPEND THE WEEKEND

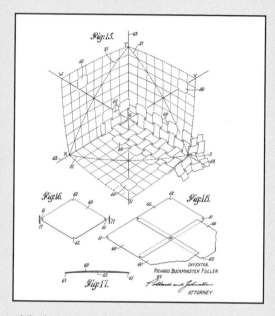

while the activity of camping itself is bucolic and pastoral. Camping synthesizes the pre-industrial and the post-industrial, losing the dirty, lumbering middle man of the industrial age itself. It promises a weekend of agrarian pleasures, returning you to the living rhythms of nature, made convenient by the elegant technologies of recent invention. Its principles of recycling and reusing, leaving no trace behind on the land, are in step with ecologically-minded ways of living, the more careful consumption of resources that will have to be at the core of 21st century global morality.

The return of camping has a wider relevance beyond merely being a nice way to spend a

The excitement's in tents

Cool Camping: England by Jonathan Knight is published by Punk Press and it lists fifty great sites to visit in England. Do not be tempted by *Cool Camping* by Laura James, as it is useless.

Since I highly recommend you to buy Jonathan Knight's *Cool Camping* book, here are my top 3 sites that do not feature in his selection.

SEVEN SISTERS COUNTRY PARK

A small walled field nestling in the lee of the chalk cliffs of the South Downs, this little site cannot be reached by car, so you will need small enough kit to walk the mile or so from the entrance to the park. The field adjoins a camping barn for backpackers so there are seats and outdoors areas for cooking. A regular bus runs from Eastbourne to Brighton and you can ask to be let off here.

TRELOAN COASTAL FARM HOLIDAYS

Seven miles away from the second home enclave of St Mawes in Cornwall, this site was once known as "Arthur's Field". The site has a long history of green idealism, set in a 1930s traditional "Nature's Way" working farm. When I was there, the farmer showed me his Shire horses which he uses for plowing and sowing the land. Then, he sat up a barbecue made out of half an oil drum overlooking the sea, and we were all invited to bring some food, a great communal act. Very helpful and interesting people in a beautiful location.

MANNIX POINT

Perched where the North Atlantic Ocean meets one fingertip of the Iveragh peninsula in Country Kerry, Ireland, this site has great views across to Knocknadobar ridge while the Valencia River flows by to become one with the bay and the ocean beyond. The owner, Mortimer, has a room set aside for peat fires and impromptu music sessions. There is also a communal kitchen and barbecue.

weekend. Its revival in our culture swims alongside other innovations, most clearly in music, where a form has evolved to fit this techno-pastoral pursuit. Called folktronica or "laptop folk", it puts the light touch of acoustic folk through the virtual mill of looping and sampling. Even the more ambient electronica has a campfire intimacy (as indicated by the title of Boards Of Canada's "Campfire Headphase"). I am no music journalist, so you'll have to excuse my amateur analysis of the evolution of folktronica. Here goes: with drum and bass, gabba and glitch techno, the music of repetitive beats went as far as it could with abrasive, dissonant noise. In the Fuse club in Brussels, I found myself dancing to little more than a man adjusting an oscillator. A few years earlier I saw the Aphex Twin put sandpaper on his turntables. His warped aesthetic, born of a certain devil-may-care attitude to drugs and a desire to *get fucked up* and *fuck things up* emulated the unnatural pace and abrasive alienation of modernity. A generation raised to love the random tickling whines of a computer game loading up on the ZX Spectrum took a boyish delight in it.

This evolution in music grew out of the festival scene. The diverse performers at Glastonbury or The Big Chill encouraged musical miscegenation while introducing a generation to the pleasures of camping. The fashion for "cool camping" is about enjoying that festival spirit between your group of friends, away from the drugs and music and merchandising stalls. The Big Chill, which is included in the England edition of Cool Camping, started out as a respite from hectic dance music. From its beginnings in the mid-1990s as a club where one recovered from dancefloor excesses, its popularity boomed even as the era of ecstasy, superclubs and Ibiza waned. Often satirized as Islington-In-The-Sun, it has thrived due to the same generational tastes that have seen the boom in organic food and Birkenstock sandles, trends for urban rusticity that have tipped into decadence.

Newer festivals such as The Green Man, the Lynton and Lynmouth Music Festival and the medieval-themed Tapestry have returned to the experimental British folk of the late 1960s and early 1970s to shake off the well-heeled hedonists. Fairport Convention, The Incredible String Band, Pentangle and the soundtrack from *The Wicker Man* are the new inspiration. Yoga-performing metropolitan types sit rapt at the feet of guitarist Burt Jansch and get off on the Jethro Tull psychedelic stylings of Circulus, before nodding to the drone noise of Voice Of The Seven Woods.

In his essay "Green Hills Of Elsewhere", Thomas Frank writes, "We are tormented by thoughts of our own impuissance [lack of power or effectiveness], our distance from the hard but real existences of our ancestors, the still-meaningful connection to nature..." The history of Western culture is threaded with new ways to overcome this impuissance, specifically the seeking out of an Other from whom we can appropriate authenticity and therefore make ourselves feel more real, and while this is undoubtedly a bold leap to make when writing about tenting, it is hard to ignore the yearning for authenticity when considering any change in the culture, since that lack, that feeling of the self as being a fake, is essentially the hunger from which our appetite for culture derives.

Where camping and the new folk movement avoids being mere authenticity mongering is its ease with both technology and Englishness. In stark contrast to the ethnic voyeurism of post-colonial literature, the gangsta rap delusion, the late 1980s yearning for a Year In Provence, or the trailer park trash stylings of trucker caps and D.A.R.E t-shirts, camping is a source of authenticity that can be a viable, realistic addition to an adult life. With camping and the new folk, the quest for authenticity has come home, as the image of English folkloric figure of the Green Man on the cover of this book attests. ◉

MAD ISLAND

How the Greek island of Leros became a modernist sanitorium. By Clare Dowdy

The mentally disabled have tended to get poor treatment in most parts of the world, and Greece was no exception – until recently.

Up until the 1980s, the Greeks liked to relocate all such undesirables on the Docedanese island of Leros. Over the years, the island evolved into a massive mental healthcare facility, where literally thousands of patients were ensconced.

Then it all became rather shocking, when the UK media did an exposé on the conditions, which proved to be nothing more than primitive. Pictures of patients manacled to beds and jolted the EU into revamping the place and its style of treatment.

Today, things couldn't be more different for the remaining patients – and not just because of the benign conditions. For some of them are dwelling in an Art Deco idyll that in other circumstances would be converted into holiday villas for the world's mid-century Modern aficionados.

For the island of Leros boasts a wealth of the most amazing Art Deco and Bauhaus architecture. It is all courtesy of the Italians, who occupied Leros for 35 years, until the Germans took over in WWII.

Mussolini envisaged Leros as the capital of his ill-fated Greek empire, and packed off a collection of architects and designers to build him a suitable metropolis. So as well as civic buildings and a church in the main town of Lakki, there are myriad military bases and officers' accommodation scattered about.

And this is where some of Leros' remaining patients are living out their days. Lepida was built as a sort of gated community for officers, complete with tranquil bay and individual single-storey dwellings or palacinos, as the Italians liked to call them.

While the impressive main naval building – the site of such mistreatment in the 1980s - is now in ruins, the palacinos are spick and span.

A stroll through Lepida these days finds patients pottering in the gardens, helping out with a bit of DIY, or just taking the air. Each palacino houses a handful of them, along with a carer. These people, who have been there all their lives, come from all over Greece.

The Aegean laps at the shore, there's bird song in the air and goats can be heard on the hillside behind. It couldn't be more therapeutic.

However, this idyll is not to last. The patients' average age is now 73, and as they die off they're not being replenished. Mental healthcare methods have changed such that treatment is offered nearer home.

So perhaps those mid-century Modernistas will get to enjoy Mussolini's Greek legacy, after all. 🌑

UNTIL RECENTLY, GREECE SENT ITS MENTALLY ILL CITIZENS TO LIVE IN THE
FASCIST-DESIGNED ART DECO BUILDINGS OF THE IDLE OF LEROS

IDLE LIVING

YURTS SO GOOD

Very cheap and surprisingly easy, living in a yurt could just be your ticket to a free life, says Dan Grace

Living in a yurt, in the countryside, rent free? Nothing more than a daydream surely? The kind of thought that surfaces in those little periods of inaction that constitutes the majority of the working day. An easily dismissed Walter Mitty-esque fantasy of a life far removed from my own, working in London, still living with my dad, on the other side of the country from my girlfriend, Ruth, and thoroughly fed up with it all. Or so I thought...

Everything changed when Ruth got a new job. Ordinarily I'm not one to celebrate such an occasion, but this was one of those rare jobs that would actually allow more freedom. She was starting work on a market garden, and the project managers agreed that we could live on the land, in a yurt, for free.

A yurt, for those of you who don't know, is basically a large wooden framed circular tent. The frame is covered by canvas and there's room to insert insulation between the structure and outer layer. With wooden doors and the possibility of solid wooden floors, plus a couple of wood burning stoves, they are closer to small cabins than tents. Traditionally the home of nomadic families of the steppes of Central Asia, they are becoming increasingly popular in the UK as a cheap and environmentally sustainable way of living.

This wasn't a snap decision. Both of us have a strong interest in green issues and had always wanted to experiment with some form of sustainable, low-impact living, but we knew that in moving into a yurt we'd be giving up a lot of our creature comforts.

Once we'd found the yurt we wanted to buy (actually two joined together to make two distinct rooms, very important when living together in confined space) we sat down and listed the pros and cons.

There were so many reasons to go for it:

DAN IN HIS YURT: YOUR OWN HOUSE IN THE COUNTRY FOR £4,000

"IT WOULD BE LIKE LIVING IN A KID'S STORY BOOK!"

1. ECONOMICS

We would own our house in the countryside for around £4,000! How many people in their mid-twenties can say that! We wouldn't be paying rent, and with no bills to speak of anything we earn could be spent on more exciting things.

2. ENVIRONMENT

Structures such as yurts leave no footprint; they have a low-impact on the environment that they are situated within. Our energy needs would be greatly reduced, and by living in such proximity to the natural world we could hopefully live a more environmentally sound lifestyle.

3. PERSONAL

Although we'll be sacrificing many of modern life's little luxuries, with no high overheads for our way of living we won't have to work as much, meaning we have more time for things that really matter; friends, family and just generally enjoying life.

4. SOCIAL

Well wouldn't you want to go stay in your friends' yurt?

5. RUTH'S OTHER REASONS

"It would be like living in a kid's story book!" and "I've always wanted to live in a round house..." Fair enough.

On the down side there's always a chance that the planners will come a-knocking. Yurts occupy a grey area in planning law and a protracted court battle could be on the cards if we're spotted by someone who doesn't take kindly to our way of life. Both Ruth and I agreed that we were happy to fight for our right to live the way we chose to. Plus there's support out there, should it come to that, in the form of organisations like Chapter 7 (www.tlio.org.uk/chapter7).

After this there still remained some nagging

doubts over the level of DIY that would be necessary for such an undertaking (no running water, no electricity, nothing to cook on until we had sorted it out), and the inverse relationship our skills had to the size of such tasks. We decided we could turn this problem into a solution and a learning experience. We knew we'd get help with the initial stages of setting the yurt up, and then we'd have plenty of time to develop and practice the skills we need.

We decided to go for it.

As I write it's been a little over a month since we moved in and I'm beginning to settle into a pattern. Life is relatively easy. I divide my day between reading on the sofa, writing on my typewriter (fun but ultimately useless), and occasional gardening whilst listening to my wind-up radio (which always winds down on the punch line of a joke).

Whilst we currently rely on camping style gas hobs to cook, a dilapidated wood burning Rayburn is sitting in the nearby barn awaiting some loving restoration and installation into the larger living room/kitchen yurt. We also have a smaller wood burner (acquired for free from the freecycle.org website!) which we hope to install in the bedroom/

bathroom yurt in time for winter, along with a bath that is currently full of tools and junk. There are also plans for solar generated electricity and hot water sometime in the future. I check my email at the local library and post is delivered to the main house by the garden.

Sleep features heavily in yurt living. Our lack of light source, other than three small candle lamps, has made us diurnal creatures. When night descends we may sit and watch the stars, but most likely we will head to the land of nod. And the next day we wake to the dawn chorus and the gentle morning light pouring in the through the roof wheel.

With only a canvas wall and some sheep's wool insulation between us and the world, the boundaries between indoor and outdoor, between us and nature are constantly blurred. Small creatures find their way inside, causing all sorts of problems. Worms and mice are the two most frequent visitors and neither cause significant trouble now that we have mouse-proofed our food boxes. Applying my limited knowledge of permaculture principles (the problem is the solution!) to this problem I wonder if it might be possible to train the mice to eat the worms, but Ruth assures me this is a stupid idea. There is a feral cat wandering about, but it sees more profit in attacking Ruth for her peanut butter sandwiches than attempting to catch a mouse.

Living as we do now is like stepping out of the world, vegetables grow on our doorstep, wild food abounds in the hedgerows and we are never short of things to do when people visit. Summer is on its way and I don't miss my old life one little bit... except maybe the baths and electricity, and I'm working on that. ◉

FILM

SLACK TO NATURE

The countryside is awful, says Paul Hamilton, and cites Withnail and I and Nuts In May to prove his point

Disregard the yearning voice echoing in your brain that pleads for a stop to modern cosmopolitan life and a return to the simple life, back to rurality and, rather than build a new Jerusalem, scamper gaily in a fresh-hewn Eden. Tish and piffle. Don't forget why we left that false idyll—namely, the countryside is awful, full of spiders and wasps, stinging nettles and poo. Why else would *I'm A Celebrity: Get Me Out Of Here* be set in a jungle? If city living is as dire and soul-sapping, as rustic sentimentalists maintain, surely that TV show would take place in a London hotel suite with well-stocked cabinets of laughing juice, DVDs and records, and hot and cold running lapdancers.

The sole inhabitants of England's green, unpleasant land are testimonies to the irreparable damage that nature does to the human psyche. They are, almost without exception, selfish, blinkered, greedy, suspicious, reactionary and staggeringly stupid. They regard all strangers as "London swankpots" who "don't understand our country ways". Anyone not part of their in-bred circle is viewed with murderous intent. The epitome of the landed gentry is florid-faced Trevor Howard, lording it bibulous in Marty Feldman's undervalued *The Last Remake Of Beau Geste* (1977) and definitively in Vivian Stanshall's crackpottery class *Sir Henry At Rawlinson End* (1980). Whereas yer average country pile would boast a lion's head fastened proud above the fireplace, Howard's walls in *Last Remake...* are packed from wainscotting to chandelier with beast bonces—tigers, hippos, rhinos, working down to food chain to kittens, shrews, lizards, perhaps even a killer ladybird or two. The entire length of Howard's hallway floor is decorated by a giraffe skin rug.

It is in Bruce Robinson's indestructible *Withnail & I* (1986) where we encounter the other end of the countryside's social ladder—the malevolent poacher, the miserable farmer, and the ex-Army-bastard-turned-publican (when Withnail bullshits that he'd served in Ireland, the rheumy-eyed major delightedly exclaims, "Ah! A crack at the Mick!").

GET OFF MY LAND: THE AUTHOR MAKES A CONVINCING FARMER

LITTER MAKES HER SHIVER: KEITH AND CANDICE-MARIE IN NUTS IN MAY,
AND THE BLOOD-LUSTING, MASOCHIST PACIFIST LAWRENCE OF ARABIA

Robinson denigrates his film as brilliant dialogue shittily shot, but it's not. He captures the true picture of the countryside—its vast, dull, damp vacuousness—unpretentiously. The great wide open has a strange effect on film directors. Ken Russell, in films fine and foul, cannot resist roaring off to his beloved Lake District to shoot scenes of religious epiphany or spiritual and physical ecstasy. David Lean started to lose his marbles with *Lawrence Of Arabia*, foregoing the warring dichotomies of TE's personality (bloodlusting masochistic pacifist) in favour of pretty but vapid shots of the desert. (Was director Vittorio De Sica mocking Lean when he played himself in *After The Fox* (1966)? On his high chair on the beach he bellows to the crew, "More sand on the desert!") Subsequent Lean epics fared no better. *Dr Zhivago* (1965) found him obsessed by snow, whereas the frankly ludicrous *Ryan's Daughter* (1971) concentrated on passing clouds. A wise decision, perhaps, since they proved more moving than anything happening below them.

KEITH IS A TIDY-BEARDED PEDANT AND FACT-GATHERER

Nuts In May (1976) is Mike Leigh's devastating analysis of the human struggle to understand, and then dominate, Mother Nature. Driving down to Dorset from Croydon in their Morris Minor are the Pratts, Keith (Roger Sloman) and Candice-Marie (Alison Steadman). Candice-Marie is a sweetly dim, lisping, lanky haired hippy, Joni Mitchell in a bobble hat and TV screen specs. Keith is a tidy-bearded pedant, an obsessive fact-gatherer, listmaker, pragmatist and windbag, with pedometer strapped to an ankle and the relevant guidebook in hand. His job, according to his wife, is "in Social Services—helping pensioners, days out". The unfortunate consequence of having to look after deaf and daft coffin-dodgers is that Keith talks to everyone in a very loud, slow, clear and deeply patronising voice.

The Pratts are in Dorset for a week's camping holiday and their differences are evident on their first day trip, to Corfe Castle. Candice-Marie is the

"WE CAN'T TAKE THREE TYPES OF FOOTWEAR, KEITH"

dreamer, the fantasist, burbling merrily away about how wonderful medieval royal feasts must have been. Keith has no time for such pleasantries: his Corfe Castle guide has numbered all the points of interest and he must whizz around and see them all. One night, in their tent (they have separate sleeping bags) Candice-Marie asks, "What are you reading, Keith?" With his back to her, he answers, *The Guinness Book Of Records*. This is the vital clue to Keith; he is a voracious collector of minutiae. He knows the Latin names for all the flowers, he can parrot-quote the rainfall figures and its effect on the landscape, but the pleasure he derives is not from being at one with the elements. Rather, it is when the actuality coincides and corresponds with what he's read about it. He is exultant in his jubilation on the beach where he finds that coastal erosion has formed a natural stairway down a cliff-face. Keith Pratt's compulsion is to control, contain, confirm and conform:

KEITH: Boots are for hiking; we wear our plimsolls for clambering about the rocks, our sandals on the beach and our boots for tramping the path in the afternoon.

CANDICE-MARIE: We can't take three types of footwear, Keith.

KEITH: You need the right tools for the job.

The holiday must follow Keith's precision planning ("the schedule"). When things disrupt his timetable and The Way He Wants Things To Be, Keith becomes a human timebomb. The fire to his short fuse arrives at the camp site in the form of two Brummie bikers, Finger, a bumfluffed gregarious ignoramus ("Look at them bleedin' bluebells," he exclaims after he's dismounted his bike, "Bleedin' millions of 'em!"), and his stack-heeled bovver bird, Honky. Whereas the Pratts are mindful of the Country Code—tut-tutting about the rubbish strewn over fields and beaches (Candice-Marie sings a self-composed lament with the refrain "Litter makes me shiver"), closing gates behind them as religiously as they chew each bite of food 72 times

—Finger and Honky are refreshingly unconcerned about the cigarettes they nonchalantly discard in their wake. Unlike the Pratts, they have no interest in geology, history or connecting on a spiritual level with the great outdoors. Finger and Honky are simply there for the craic—getting outside of a few ales and having a game of arrows in a village boozerie. They can't even pitch their tent correctly. It is when Finger gathers branches with the intention of building a fire so he and Honky can cook some bangers and beans for breakfast that Keith goes wild. Ignoring his protestations that such a fire contravenes the Country Code, is an air pollutant and dangerous (Finger has set the firewood only a foot or two away from his tent), Keith grabs the largest of Finger's branches and, poking it violently and threateningly at his nemesis, begins screaming and hollering. He has finally lost his capacity to reason; he has become a wild beast of the forest.

Keith Pratt is no easy cartoon caricature, no obvious Pythonesque grotesque. He is a multi-layered tragi-comic creation. Roger Sloman has never bettered this performance. Seeing *Nuts In May* and *Withnail & I* once again, the message sings out pure and clear: Stay out of the country. It's not natural. ☺

FURTHER VIEWING;
Being There (1979)
I Know Where I'm Going (1945)
I Love You, Alice B. Toklas (1968)
She'll Be Wearing Pink Pyjamas (1987)
Johnny Weissmuller's Tarzan flicks
The Emerald Forest (1982)
Deliverance (1972)

FOURTEEN YEARS, 37 BACK ISSUES

1: August '93
SOLD OUT
Dr Johnson
Terence McKenna

2: Nov~Dec '93
SOLD OUT
Homer Simpson
Will Self

3: Jan~Feb '94
£8.00
Bertrand Russell
Charles Handy

4: April~May '94
SOLD OUT
Kurt Cobain
Matt Black

5: July~Aug '94
SOLD OUT
Douglas Coupland
Jerome K Jerome

6: Sept~Oct '94
SOLD OUT
Easy Listening
Richard Linklater

7: Dec~Jan '95
SOLD OUT
Sleep
Gilbert Shelton

8: Feb~Mar '95
SOLD OUT
Jeffrey Bernard
Robert Newman

9: May~June '95
SOLD OUT
Suzanne Moore
Positive Drinking

10: July~Aug '95
SOLD OUT
Damien Hirst
Will Self

11: Sept~Oct '95
£4.00
Keith Allen
Dole Life

12: Nov~Dec '95
£4.00
Bruce Robinson
All Night Garages

13: Jan~Feb '96
SOLD OUT
Stan Lee
Life As A Kid

14: Mar~Apr '96
£4.00
Bruce Reynolds
Will Self

15: May~Jun '96
SOLD OUT
Hashish Killers
Alex Chilton

16: Aug~Sept '96
SOLD OUT
John Michel
World Poker

17: Nov~Dec '96
SOLD OUT
John Cooper Clarke
Cary Grant

18: Spring '97
SOLD OUT
Thomas Pynchon
Ivan Illich

19: Summer '97
£4.00
Psychogeography
Henry Miller

20: Winter '97
SOLD OUT
Howard Marks
Kenny Kramer

21: Feb~March '98
SOLD OUT
The Gambler
Bez

23: June~July '98
SOLD OUT
Summer Special
Tim Roth

24: Aug~Sep '98
SOLD OUT
Krazy Golf
David Soul

22: April~May '98
SOLD OUT
Alan Moore
Alex James

MAN'S RUIN
25: Winter 1999
£15
The first book-format Idler, featuring Louis Theroux's Sick Notes, Will Self, Howard Marks, Adam and Joe and Ken Kesey

PARADISE
26: Summer 2000
£5
Jonathan Coe meets David Nobbs, Nicholas Blincoe on Sherlock Holmes, Tiki Special, Iain Sinclair on the London Eye

THE FOOL
27: Winter 2000
£5
Village Idiots, World Of Pain, Arthur Smith's diary, The Big Quit, James Jarvis's World of Pain, John Lloyd

RETREAT
28: Summer 2001
£10
Louis Theroux meets Bill Oddie, Jonathan Ross meets Alan Moore, Alex James meets Patrick Moore, plus Andrew Loog Oldham

HELL 29: Winter 2001
£10
Crass founder Penny Rimbaud, Crap Jobs Special, Boredom Section, New fiction from Niall Griffiths, Mark Manning, Billy Childish

LOVE 30: Summer 2002
£10
Louis Theroux meets Colin Wilson, Johnny Ball on Descartes, Crap Towns, Devon Retreat, Chris Yates interview, Marchesa Casati

REVOLUTION 31: Winter 2002
£10
Dave Stewart, Black Panthers, Saint Monday, Allotments, Riots, Introducing the Practical Idler section

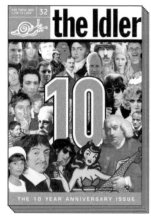

ANNIVERSARY 32:
Winter 2003

£10

Damien Hirst on why cunts sell
shit to fools; Marc Bolan; the
pleasures of the top deck; Walt
Whitman; happiness

LADIES OF LEISURE 33:
Spring 2004

£10

Clare Pollard is sick of shopping;
Girls on bass; the wit and
wisdom of Quentin Crisp;
Barbara Ehrenreich

THE FOOD ISSUE 34:
Winter 2004

£10

Joan Bakewell on life as a
freelancer; Bill Drummond's
soup adventure; The Giro
Playboy; Falconry; why
supermarkets are evil and
Jerome K Jerome

35: WAR ON WORK
Spring 2005

£10

Keith Allen's A to Z of life;
Raoul Vaneigem interview;
Jeremy Deller's Folk Art;
Dan Kieran's Seven Steps To
The Idle Life; Chris Donald, Peter
Doherty and more Crap Jobs

**36: YOUR MONEY OR YOUR
LIFE**
Winter 2005

£10

Mutoid Waste Company;
Edward Chancellor on credit;
Penny Rimbaud; Jay Griffiths;
A Hitch Hiker's Guide; the Guilds;
Chris Donald

37: CHILDISH THINGS
Spring 2006

£10

Childcare for The Lazy;
Michael Palin; Bertrand Russell;
Free-Range Education;
Running away to Join
the Circus

THE VIEW FROM THE SOFA

An industrial dream turns into a rural nightmare for

Greg Rowland

CHRIS WATSON

Like so many of us, I had often dreamt about owning a massive heavy industrial complex. Large steel plants, particularly in the regions-de-jour of Tyneside and Pontypridd, always provided a welcome retreat from the endless blithe verdure of one's country estate. Of course, after all the recent media infatuation with 3.5 metre magnate-tensile girders, demand had been exceptionally high.

Nevertheless, I had set my sites on the charming Corus Steel Processing Plant on the Tyne. Not only did they produce the now almost obligatory 3.5 metre magnate-tensile girders, but it was whispered that they were about to start working on a fabulous 1.25mm steel corded-wire mesh—guaranteed to be the absolute must-have for next season's giddy round of construction and infrastructure development shows. It was going to be so very beyond the New Black that it was as though a thousand galaxies had simultaneously imploded and created a black hole so powerful that it sucked in all the light in the universe, including all the light that ever might exist in an infinity of hypothetical parallel dimensions.

So, there I was, waving my cheque book at the factory gates, as the stunningly beautiful local artisans thronged cheerfully onwards. They charmingly regaled me with the traditional local greetings of "coont" and "wan-ha".

Yet, glancing at the morning's paper, I saw something that turned my idyllic dreams into a perfect nightmare. According to Melvinna Wrigley-Smint's column, large industrial plants (and even medium-sized factories for God's sake!) were significantly contributing to something called "Global Warming". Hence ownership of such edifices was no longer *de rigueur*. Even that sexy puffy-faced elf David Cameron had said so.

Trudging back to the grim 90 acres of non-steel producing woodland glens and croquet lawns of my drab little country estate, I began to ponder on this whole global warming hoo-hah. Now, don't get me wrong, I'm all for Johnny Foreigner making a home on our shores. And I like a fine curry as much as the next man. However, when he brings his weather with him, I feel I simply must object. I have made a great personal sacrifice by relinquishing my dream of owning a large industrial steel plant. I'm certainly doing my bit for global warming. So the least other people can do is leave their hot weather at home, where it belongs, in the hot countries. Foreign weather? No, thank you very much. ◉